MW01616333

PRAISE FOR *DESPERATE HOODWIV*

"Let's just say this sassy, sexy, streetwise story could some butt over on Wisteria Lane." (Listed as REQUIR READING)

—*New York*

"A wonderfully written story with colorful characters will keep you flipping the pages—I loved it."

—K'wan, *Essence* bestselling aut

"*Desperate Hoodwives* is a wonderfully written novel is sassy, smart, and unadulterated!"

—Danielle Santiago, *Essence* bestselling aut

"The authors, who also publish under Niobia Bryant Adrianne Byrd, hold back little in this cautionary dripping with sex, vice, and yearning."

—*Publishers Wee*

"Erotic and explosive, *Desperate Hoodwives* is well-writ and I could not put it down."

—RAW Sis

Also by Meesha Mink and De'nesha Diamond:

Desperate Hoodwives
Shameless Hoodwives

The Hood Life

A Bentley Manor Tale

Meesha Mink and
De'nesha Diamond

A TOUCHSTONE BOOK

PUBLISHED BY SIMON & SCHUSTER

NEW YORK LONDON TORONTO SYDNEY

Touchstone
A Division of Simon & Schuster, Inc.
1230 Avenue of the Americas
New York, NY 10020

This book is a work of fiction. Names, characters, places, and incidents either are products of the author's imagination or are used fictitiously. Any resemblance to actual events or locales or persons, living or dead, is entirely coincidental.

Designed by Carla Jayne Little

Manufactured in the United States of America

ISBN: 978-1-60751-375-9

Rest in peace, Momma. You are my angel and I love you.
—Meesha

To: Tushonda Whitaker and Elliott Goins.
Thanks for holding me down.
—De'nesha

Prologue

Miz Cleo

Summertime is hell in Bentley Manor. The Georgia heat is enough to drive you mad and folks around here start actin' like they's ain't got no sense. I've seen a lot in my seventy-three years and I've experienced pain I wouldn't wish on my worse enemy. But heartache is nothing new in Bentley Manor. In fact, it comes with the territory.

As I sit out here on this stoop with my best friend Osceola Washington by my side, I look around this U-shaped complex marveling how it's getting harder and harder to tell the days apart. I've been living here since June of '69. Lost my husband in '71. After raising four children, one grandchild, I'm now strugglin' to raise my great-grandbaby.

It's hard.

And I'm tired.

Over the years, or rather, over the decades, Atlanta has gone through some changes. Bentley Manor started off as regular apartment complex, but in the late '70s it was the ghetto, in the late '80s the projects. Now, it's the hood.

This place is crawling with the worst of the worst and I've seen my fair share of pimps, dealers, playas, and killers. Too many, in fact.

Some wonder how people survive places like Bentley Manor. To that, I can only shrug my shoulders and ask "what choice do we have?"

The hood life is all we know. . . .

The Pimp

Pussy is big business.

And I'm a businessman—a damn good one. Yeah, I dibble and dabble in a few other things. Who doesn't? If a nigga wants to carve himself a piece of the American pie, he's got to get his hustle on. You feel me? I'm sure you do. Tavon Johnson is the name and pussy is my game.

'Course, on the streets they call me Sweet Diamondtrim Johnson. Diamonds are my trademarks. So much so that each of my girls keeps their pussy shaved and sport diamond tattoos inches above their clits. I want my customers to know they're getting diamond quality.

If you're wondering how I got into this business, I guess you could say I sort of fell into it. I popped my first cherry at twelve. Her name was Renee Collins. I swear to this day that she has the sweetest pussy a nigga ever tasted. And 'course I bragged this shit to my best friend

Destin. Bragged so much that he promised to give me his allowance for a full month if I let him have a go at Renee himself.

Being an entrepreneurial nigga even at that age, I took the deal—only if I was allowed to watch. Hell, Destin's parents gave him five dollars a week, and in '82 you have no idea how many hours of pinball that gave a nigga.

Renee was pissed, but it had been easy to convince her fuckin' Destin was her chance to prove how much she loved me. I gotta tell ya: watching her in action with my best friend was an incredible high. Watching her do a few more boys behind the schoolyard and under the gym bleachers convinced me that I really did love her.

All in all, it was just another reason in a long list of why I married her. For the record, she still has the sweetest pussy I've ever tasted.

So what's your fantasy? I have every kind of ho you can imagine: Black, white, Puerto Rican or Asian. You name it, I got it. You want a streetwalker, a glamorous escort, a porno star, or maybe you're one of those down-low brothers. Don't matter. I got a few dicks on the payroll, too. It's all pussy to me.

Being in the biz for a quarter, I've seen it all. You can whip them, tie them up, and you can even piss on them, if that's your thing. It's all negotiable. But don't get it twisted; pimpin' ain't easy.

From time to time I catch whiff of a few girls talking 'bout how they're going to leave. I laugh at that shit.

Where the fuck are they going to go? What are they going to do, shovel fries at McDonald's, convince one of their johns to marry them? C'mon. Once a ho always a ho.

Besides, they're not going to find another nigga that's going to treat them better than I do. Like the Disciple Curtis Mayfield said: "I'm their momma, I'm their daddy, I'm that nigga in the alley."

I'd be lyin' if I said from time to time one doesn't leave the nest . . . but they come back. They always come back. Bottom line: they love me, they hate me, they love me. I can live with that.

As long as the bitch has my money.

That's the key to my success. While all these ashy Negroes scramble around tryna turn everybody and their momma into crackheads, I'm building an empire off the best commodity there is—and I do mean the best.

From rap stars to government officials, I keep the juices and the money flowing.

I grew up poor and I ain't never going back. Fuck that shit.

Of course, I don't whine and moan like most. A sad story in Bentley Manor is a dime a dozen. We don't need anyone to tell us that we got the short end of the stick. The question is: How are you going to play the hand you were dealt? Me? I didn't choose pimpin'. Pimpin' chose me. The first girl I had to protect was my own damn momma.

Now, some men have a problem havin' a ho for a

momma. Not me. I recognize my momma did what she had to do to put food on the table for five children (all of us with different daddies), and I ain't got nothin' but mad respect for her game. Of course, for a long time, she lied to us and to herself by telling us that the men who marched in and out of our apartment were good friends of the family—friends who left money on the bedside table after they "wrestled naked in her bed."

Once, my older brother, Kadrian, and I hid under her bed and found out what really went on in that room when she closed the door. And let me tell ya: Momma had skills. Niggas would call out her name like she was Christ Almighty. A lot of them brought her gifts and some even thought to bring us something, too.

For a few years, we were the envy of most our friends: sportin' the new canvas sneaks, rockin' the latest dookey rope chains and carrying the biggest boom boxes imaginable. Then crack hit the streets and Momma got hooked.

First, she tried to maintain, but that didn't last long.

Soon, thugs and drug dealers replaced the niggas with money. Our fly-ass gear disappeared about as fast as the food in the refrigerator. Within three months, Momma was out on the streets, offering to suck dicks just for a hit. Some started beating on her. The strange thing was she acted like she didn't care. All she wanted was to get high.

Well, I cared. And nobody was gonna whup my momma's ass right in front of me or my hood. So me and my brother started looking out for her—collecting her money, making sure that she got paid.

Hell, we had to eat.

This arrangement pretty much went on through our teen years. But all our protecting couldn't prevent her from coming up HIV positive a couple years ago. That fuckin' sex fiend Junior spread that shit to a lot of girls when he was stayin' up at Bentley Manor. If his wife hadn't capped his ass, I sure the fuck would have.

But live and learn. All *my* girls get tested on the regular and I screen their johns like the motherfuckin' FBI. What can I say? I have to protect my investment.

My three sisters, Candy, Brandi, and Cherry, followed our mother's footsteps. They call themselves Video Vixens now, but you know, a ho by any other name . . .

Me, I keep doing what I'm good at: protecting and selling pussy.

My big brother, Kadrian, didn't make it out of his teens. He got caught up in gangbanging and took a couple of bullets to the chest. Not a day goes by when I don't think about him, wishing he was here counting this money with me.

Pimpin' ain't like what you see in the movies. Sure there are some guys who walk around draped in gaudy jewelry, iron-pressed curls, and dress like it's 1972, but those are little boys fulfilling their *Superfly* fantasies. Pimpin' is a business and I dress like any other CEO of a Fortune 500 company. Ten-thousand-dollar suits from William Fioravanti, Caraceni, and Oxxford, with a little tasteful bling from De Beers and my ass look ready for the cover of *GQ* every day.

"I'm sorry, sir," Anderson, my driver, says over his shoulder. "Doesn't look like this traffic is gonna let up anytime soon."

I pull my gaze from a So-So Def billboard to meet his eyes in the Bentley's rearview mirror. "Take your time. I'm not in a hurry."

He nods and I return my attention to that ridiculous billboard and continue reflecting over my life—all thirty-seven years of it.

It wasn't easy, but I finally got my girls off the street corner. Found safer ways for us all to do our jobs. Yeah, I own a couple of private strip clubs, book a couple of booty-shaking dancers for rap stars and keep a hefty amount of city government officials sexed up so good that they stay off my back.

All of this is good money, but it all pales in comparison to what I make off the Red Light District Web site: videos, CD-ROMS, DVD, Video on Demand, and sex toys. Again, name your pleasure and I can hook you up.

After all, I'm a freak, too.

At long last, my nut sack starts tingling. I close my eyes and loll my head back to give the mouth around my cock a little more room.

"That's it. Don't stop," I moan and pump my hips. Out of all my girls, including Renee, no one sucks my dick the way Destiny does. No one. I place my hand on the back of her long flowing weave and bob her head down to a faster rhythm.

Shit. I'm ready to come and I know this trick is gonna swallow my full load and then keep sucking until my toes curl.

"Aw, shit. You nasty motherfucker," I growl as I hold her head down and finally explode into that wonderful mouth.

Like a true sex soldier, Destiny keeps going and I start to inch up the leather upholstery because my shit is suddenly sensitive. Finally, I have to shove her off and try to catch my breath.

Destiny chuckles and reaches for her purse to retrieve her compact and lipstick. "I don't know how Renee is still number one when she can't deep throat like I do."

I tuck my dick back into my pants and stare at her as she fixes her makeup. Well, technically, she is a he and quite possibly the best damn transvestite I've ever seen.

I don't question my sexuality—and nobody else does either. I do whateva gets me off. The world would be a better place if everyone did the same.

Destiny snaps her compact closed and smiles. "Feel better, baby?"

"As always," I say and catch Anderson's nosy gaze in the rearview mirror. For a fleeting moment, I'm sure I see disgust reflect in his eyes.

"Destiny," I say, maintaining eye contact with my driver. "Climb up front and hook Anderson up for me."

"That's not necessary, Mr. Johnson," Anderson sputters immediately.

"I know it's not necessary, but what can I say, I'm a generous guy. And I don't like it when people turn down my generosity—especially people who work for me."

Without a doubt this nigga understands that his options are to get his dick wet or get the fuck out in the middle of rush-hour traffic.

Destiny watches the exchange in amused silence and when I give her a small wink, she climbs over into the front seat and unzips Anderson's pants.

"Well, you ain't got much to work with. Do you, honey?" Destiny asks.

Anderson's face darkens.

I can't help but laugh. "And make sure you don't wreck my shit."

This time, horror covers Anderson's face and I keep on laughing.

A couple of slurps and this motherfucker lays on the brakes and starts cumin'.

"Damn, man. I barely got started." Destiny drops her fake feminine voice for a sec and her masculine bass fills the car.

Anderson looks as if he'd just been raped or some shit. Maybe he's stunned that he enjoyed the experience. Like I said: Destiny's the best.

Nearly an hour later, we roll through Bentley Manor's wrought-iron gate. My attention is instantly drawn to the trembling crackheads and hustling dope dealers. And sure enough, sitting out on their concrete stoop, in the center of the U-shaped complex, are Miz Cleo and Miz Osceola. Hell, I can feel their glares before I even get out of the car.

Fuck 'em. They don't like me and I sure as hell don't give a shit about them.

Ain't a damn thing changed about this motherfucker since I grew up here. It's just as dirty and grimy as ever.

Anderson hops his fat ass out the driver's seat and quickly opens my back door. I climb out, pose a bit so everyone can take their time eyeing my summer-white suit and customized bling.

What's the point of having money if you can't show it off?

A few dealers bob their heads in greeting and way too many underage girls try to catch my attention. But I ain't lookin' at shit that ain't eighteen.

Period.

Destiny starts to climb out of the car, but I quickly tell her, "Stay put. I'll be back in a sec." I clutch the head of my silver-handled cane (one stereotype I won't give up) and stroll like the pimp I am toward my old childhood building.

When Momma answers her door, I have to hand it to her: she's looking pretty good. It's clear that she's been keeping up with her HIV cocktails.

"Hey, baby." She tightens the belt on her robe and leans up on her tiptoes to deliver a kiss against my cheek.

"I didn't know you were coming by today."

"I always come by on the fifteenth," I say, strolling through the door. I'm not the least surprised to see a john sitting on the couch. After all, Momma is always gonna be Momma.

"Well, I guess I better get going," the dude says, jumping to his feet and scrambling toward the door.

I stop him cold. "Aren't you forgetting something?" I ask.

He glances at Momma and then back at me while getting all flustered.

"Uh, yeah." He reaches for his wallet in his back pocket and peels off a couple of Benjamins. "My bad."

I just nod, but I make sure he reads in my expression that shit wasn't cool.

"I catch you later, Angel," the man says and quickly races out the door.

I turn my gaze toward Momma. "Angel?"

"What? Don't I look like an Angel to you?"

I just laugh at that shit. Momma ain't ever gonna change. And neither will I. "All right, Angel. You got my money?"

2

The Dealer

"Mornin', Daddy."

Lying in the middle of my silk-covered, king-sized bed, I look over to the left at Suga smiling up at me and then over to my right at her sister Spyce, giving me an identical smile. Twins.

I smile like the cocky motherfucker I am because a nigga ain't really lived until he had two big-tittie freak bitches willing to double-team his dick. Fuck Charlie, I got the real deal angels right here waiting to fuck and suck me right.

Each one strokes their tongue across one of my nipples and my dick stands up like a fucking soldier making the silk sheet rise right on up. I press my hands to the back of their heads and even though we all just met last night, these bitches know to suck deeper on my nipples. My dick's so hard it's aching like a motherfucker. I ain't gone lie, these chicks might make me nut up my damn sheets.

I close my eyes and lick my lips while I fight like hell to hold off cumming. Either Suga or Spyce wraps their hand around that long, thick motherfucker to stroke it like they tryna draw milk. I hiss in pleasure and my hips arch up off the bed as they both giggle softly against my chest.

I know I should've got them the hell out of my apartment as soon as I sprayed my nut into both of their mouths, but after the fucking these chicks put on me I couldn't do shit *but* sleep. I open one eye and look over at the Ralph Lauren digital clock on the dresser as I reach down their smooth brown bodies to palm two of the softest breasts I ever fucked with. Ten a.m. Shit.

From the second I laid eyes on them in Visions nightclub and they both gave me the eye back I knew I had to have them. I'm an ass and tittie man all the way and these bangin'-ass bitches had both with none of that extra stomach and stretch-mark bullshit.

They both moan as I use my fingertips to tease their nipples. I have to get some of their pussies before I roll out for the day. Fuck it.

"Suck my dick." I didn't direct that shit to one or the other. It really didn't matter as long as I felt my tip wet soon.

They both shift from my arms to get on their knees on the bed and lick from the base to the thick tip. They alternate one to the other, wrapping their thick lips around my dick to suck deeply.

One and then the other. Back and forth. Each suck

deeper and deeper until they are deep-throating me. I can feel their tonsils on my shit. Damn!

"That dick good, ain't it?" I ask them thickly, my eyes half closed as I look at them do their work.

"Uhm-humm," they moan in unison.

I cross my feet, put my hands behind my head, and just kick back enjoying my life as these chicks handle a dick the way it should forever and always be handled.

Soft hands spread my legs wide and soon one set of cool lips suck my balls into her mouth while her twin easily handles all ten of my curved inches. I shiver like a straight-up bitch, but fuck it. This shit feels good as a motherfucker and their moans is turning me the fuck on even more. My toes curl and my stomach gets tight as hell as I feel my dick get harder in one of their mouths.

"Hey, Suga, this dick gone cum," Spyce whispers against my tip. "Want some?"

"Damn right."

My doorbell sounds off just as I bite my bottom lip to keep from hollering out as my dick pumps like a fucking gun filling their mouths with my cum. My heart is beating and sweat is covering my body as tongues and lips suck and lick up every bit of my nut.

The doorbell sounds again as I lay stretched out in the bed trying to breathe so that my motherfuckin' ass didn't stroke out or some shit. As good as they took care of that dick, I know who is at the door. It's time for business.

With one last slap to their identical plush-ass cheeks,

I sit up. "Ladies, this is good. Shit, damn good, but I got work to do."

"We feel you, Kaseem."

"Go make that money, honey."

Seconds later I'm missing the soft feel of their bodies sandwiching my body. I roll out of bed and hop to my feet as they begin to dress in the same skintight Baby Phat jean outfits that drew my ass to them last night.

I slip on one of my thick-ass Hilfiger terrycloth robes and stick my feet into matching plaid slippers. "Stay here," I tell them, before leaving my bedroom and closing the door behind me.

My three-bedroom apartment is laid the fuck out like I hired some Martha Stewart type of bitch to decorate my shit. But I picked it all out myself. The chocolate leather furniture, the African wood carvings on the wall, the black top of the line appliances. All of it was all me. It's what I'm used to so there's no way I could settle for anything less. And since money is never an issue, whatever I want I get.

I cross the polished hardwood floors to open the front door. My best friend and right hand-man, Usher, strolls in wearing an oversized thick-ass T-shirt. I know he hot as a motherfucker in this summer heat but fuck it, we do what we do.

As he pulls the shirt over his bald head, I open the fridge and pull out a bottle of apple juice to take a deep swig from. By the time I finish my drink he has unstrapped two money belts from around his solid waist and dropped them onto the smoky glass dining-room table.

One hundred thousand dollars.

I reach across the table and without a word spoken my nigga gives me some dap and one of his fucked-up, crooked-tooth grins. Usher look like a bulldog from his face to the thick and solid build of body. Fuck it, what this motherfucker lacked in looks he made up for in loyalty. We been friends for the longest and he hasn't ever let me down.

I shrug and pick up the belts to hold in one of my strong hands. I love money. Always have. Always will. Even this chump change got a nigga like me happy as a motherfucker. And the hustle—*my* hustle—makes sure the pockets stay fat.

Hustling is all I know how to do. Shit, I ain't the only one. Whether you in corporate America, busting your ass on a blue-collar nine to five, or going for yours in the hood, *everybody* got a hustle. Mine is dope. Right, wrong, or indifferent, it is what it is, and I make it do what it do. I don't gangbang. I never killed a motherfucker. I hardly ever been in a fight. I ain't angry and dangerous and all that "stereotypical shit." I sling dope. Period.

And this dope game has been good to me.

Good money. Good friends. Good life.

The Hood Life. Fuck it.

Anything I want is at the tip of my fingers, a phone call away, a shout of my voice, or the snap of my fingers. And

I live my life to the fullest. The flyest gear. The dopest bitches. The baddest rides.

I love my boy Maleek like a brother, but I have to admit when the feds shut down his multistate operation last year, I slipped right on in and upped my game from weed (which still did me damn good all these years) to pushing that hard weight. Hell, somebody had to meet the demands with the best supply and with Maleek's help I have the best fucking connections in place to run these streets. In return, I set aside a nice stash of money for him (that no one including his wife, Aisha, knew about) and I got word to him straight the fuck up, that his precious wife, Miss High and Mighty, was selling that sweet-ass pussy all over Atlanta while he was locked up.

Truth?

I can't even front that I was mad that she rather sell it than give it to me. Oh, I wanted that pussy bad as a motherfucker. Wife of my friend or not, if Aisha had let me just lick that, then Maleek's ass would just have to share on the low. Hell, it wasn't like Maleek didn't fuck around on her.

Fuck it, I *still* want to punish that pussy. Make her feel what the fuck she was missing. The street patrol said she was still runnin' the pussy game but who knew if that was true or not. She slipped off the radar like a motherfucker but—

"Hey, Kas."

What the fuck?

I glance over at Usher as my front door slams closed and my girl Quilla walks in with the key I gave her swinging from her hands.

"Damn," I swear as I get over to her quick as a motherfucker. Any other Sunday her ass in church all morning. Nothing but that radar of *hers* told her I was somewhere near some pussy other than *hers*.

"Whaddup, baby girl," I say, even as I see Usher grab the money belts from the table. I check her out real quick before I grab her by the waist and turn her to steer her sexy black ass back to the front door.

Oh, Quilla finer than a motherfucker with her dark complexion and long curly weave down her back, but right now she's more inconvenient than anything. Fuck the smooth laid-back demeanor, this bitch flips with a quickness when she catch me trickin'. Quilla will forget her designer outfit—which I know cost three grand, since I bought it—and try and tear up my damn apartment. She got a scanner on this dick and the last thing I need is for her to catch the Fuck You Good twins up in here.

That's why I usually never bring bitches back to my apartment. Never. I don't know why I fucked with that shit last night.

"You skipped church?" I ask as I feel her resisting my hand on her elbow.

"I'm on my way. Why? You got a problem with me stopping by?" she asks, her neck already going in a different damn direction from her head.

"Me and Usher got some business to handle and you know I don't have you in my shit like that."

She looks over her shoulder and pierces Usher with one of her hazel cat-shaped eyes. "Yeah, what the fuck ever, Kas."

I open the front door and keep guiding her ass right on out. "Quilla, this ain't that time for that dumb shit. I ain't gone let nobody fuck with my money and you know that," I tell her, trying to go hard and shit. "Whatever I lose from you playing the pussy detective I will take from all that shit you ask me for. So what you wanna do?"

She smiles and her dimples that I love come right on out as she gets up on the tip of her Gucci heels and gives me a deep kiss. "I'll be back after church," she whispers against my lips before she turns and walks out the door with one last stare at me. "Don't play with me."

I'm just glad my shit don't taste like the twins' pussy. And the thought of the twins makes me decide to get rid of Usher too. Hell, he done made the drop. I can chill with his ass later.

"Yo, Ush, I'm going back to bed. I'll get up with you later." I even throw in a stretch.

Usher just shakes his head. "Man, you can shit Quilla but don't even try that bullshit with me."

I laugh because he's right. Feeling cocky as a motherfucker, I tie my robe a little tighter and strut my ass to my bedroom to open it wide. Suga and Spyce are dressed and sitting on the edge of the bed waiting to be told what to do.

I look over my shoulder as Usher walks up to me and slaps me on the back. "You a bad motherfucker."

I don't say nothing else because there isn't shit else to be said. Not even good-bye. Usher know what the fuck is up.

Before the front door even closes behind him, I drop my robe. They're already here and the coast is clear for a second. Might as well enjoy it. Fuck it.

Suga drops right to her knees and makes my dick hard as hell in her mouth as Spyce spreads my ass and licks a trail around the hole.

Stretching my arms wide I let my head drop back and enjoy myself. Damn, life is good as hell.

3

The Playa

Life is so fuckin' good . . . *especially* for a fine mother-fucker like me. Just twenty-eight, high yellow, gray eyes, good hair, toned body, and a big dick—oh, I'm *the* shit and I know it. I've always known it and there ain't shit in this world I want that I can't get, especially if what I want belongs to a woman. Money. Clothes. Jewelry. Three hots and a cot. And for sure, pussy. Pussy. And more pussy.

Ain't too many men that can twist a woman's legs like a pretzel and then lay that pipe so good that she forget how I had her hemmed up.

When I say jump my bitches ask how high.

When I say suck this dick they ask how deep.

When I say give me money their *only* question better be how much.

I roll out of the bed and reach for my creased brown

Dickies pants from the floor. A nigga was ready to go for real.

"Where you going, Rhak?"

I blow out some air as I pull on my shit before I turn to look down at her. Not that looking in her face or calling the bitch by her name mean a damn thing. To me all these tricks and chicks is one and the same. No matter how much they suck and fuck me ain't none of these tricks mean more to me than the other. Not even my girl, Shaterica.

"I'm headin' back to the crib, baby," I tell her in my smoothest voice. (I call them all baby to keep from saying the wrong name at the wrong damn time. Don't hate the playa. . . .)

Taira flips the covers back and shows me her brickhouse body covered by the tightest, smoothest, and darkest skin ever. *Humph.* Her pussy is just as tight.

She *thinks* we have a future. The bitch is straight crazy. Taira ain't the settle-down-with kinda chick. She can't cook. Her apartment shady as hell when it comes to bein' clean and she got more kids than the projects got roaches, but her sugar walls can grip my dick tighter than a motherfucker that's pissed the hell off. *Humph.* I ain't forgot 'bout that whole hooker-to-housewife shit. But . . . if it took a few soft words and a few more hard strokes to get that pussy *when* I want it and *how* I want it then fuck it, Taira can think whatever the hell she want.

"I gotta go but I'll get up with you tomorrow," I tell

her with "the look"—deep stare, hard jaw, head tilted slightly to the side with a wink followed by half a smile. It gets these bitches every time.

Like clockwork "the look" turns her frown up the fuck side down. (I will be eternally grateful to my uncle LeRon for teaching me that and some more shit that keeps this true playa for real in true pussy forever.)

I stroll my ass right out her junky bedroom and ignore the hell out her snot-nose kids sittin' in the livin' room as I walk out the house forgettin' her with as much ease as I please. I done got what I want from her ass. My dick done got good and wet and my pockets are a little fatter. I finger the crisp hundred dollar bill she gave me. She thinks of it as a loan and I know it's payment for services rendered. Translation: she might as well kiss this bill good-bye. Besides, my girl been naggin' me to pay half on the car note so now I can get *her* the fuck off my back.

I'm singin' along with the radio as I drive up Piedmont in my black Honda Accord—well, it's Shaterica's, but fuck it, what's hers is mine. All she ever does is hand me the keys with a smile and I'm up out of Bentley Manor quick as shit. I drive it, fuck in it, pull new bitches in it, and do what the hell I please in it. Just last week I drove over to this little white chick I fuck with over in Buckhead. I slipped and spent the night with that bitch and my girl was mad as hell and straight mean-muggin' me when I dragged my ass through the door the next mornin'. I shot her a lie about gettin' effed up and fallin' asleep on one of my homeboys' couch—picture *that* shit really happenin'. Shit, I ain't one of them cruddy down-low brothers. My name is Rhakmon, not Junior.

Not that I don't care about my lady. She real good to me and I know it. Even though she say I don't recognize all the shit she does for me, that's her job. She knew that when she filled out the application and whenever her ass feel like she can't handle what the fuck it takes to be my girl then I'll fire her. She know what's up.

I check the clock on the dash. It's 10:18.

Shaterica works as a nursing assistant at some old folks' home from eleven at night 'til eleven in the mornin'. She needed her car to get to work and one thing I don't fuck with is holdin' a bitch up from carryin' her ass to work. I need her money and my free time to do me. For real.

I steer the car with one hand and try my best to reach in the glove compartment for one of my blunts. Ready-made and rolled to please.

If there is two things God created for this playa's pleasure then it's pussy and weed. Mix a good fuckin' smoke with some smokin' good pussy and . . . hot damn!

I sink deeper into the driver's seat just as I stick the blunt in my mouth and light it. That nut I bust and this blunt is gonna lay my ass out for the night. This one time Shaterica's jealous ass won't have to hunt me the fuck up. A nigga's bed was callin'.

I turned at the next corner with a little Snoop playin'

from the CD player. Perfect music to ride and get high. I rode down a damn near deserted block that I know all too well—less police traffic. I felt like gettin' effed up not frisked.

As I pull to a red light I tilt my head up to blow a stream of smoke up through the open sunroof. I look around me and I smile all cocky and shit at the sight of the small brick house on the corner. I used to fuck this bitch who rented that shitty little motherfucker. Big Butt Belinda.

I'm laughing at the memory of her suckin' the hell out of my dick while I used a stack of dollar bills to make it rain on that ho.

My smile fades as the front door opens and I look into the face of this mark-ass nigga named Onthario. A bitch-ass name for a bitch-ass fool.

I don't give a fuck about this clown and I know he could care less about me. Shit, we ain't got no choice but to hate each other. . . .

"Yes, Rhakmon. Do that shit, boy. Do it!"

And just because Big Butt Belinda asked me so damn nicely, I did do it. I used my hands to press her thick brick-house legs high into the air until her sweet ass spread before me like a buffet as I worked my dick inside her walls. To the left, to the right, back to the left and back to the right. With each stroke she quivered until her ass and thighs wiggled and jiggled in a thousand different directions. The tight heat of her walls made my dick harder. Well, there was never a good reason to let a hard dick go to waste so I worked my back until my sweat had both us of wet from head to toe. She did enough hollering and squirming to let me know she appreciated the extra effort.

Loving to hear a bitch beg for this dick I jerk my hips back pulling it out of her wetness with a swoosh.

And like clockwork . . .

"No, Daddy, no," she whined, biting her bottom lip in frustration as she jerked her hips upward to try and capture my thick dick with her pussy lips.

I look down into her face—a face I just saw for the first time three hours ago at Cascade, the local skating rink. As I leaned down to suck her tongue and kissed her I demanded, "Say please."

"Please, Daddy, please."

I swooped right back on in to pop that coochie some more. Humph, *I walked into Cascade to do some freestyle skating with my homeboys and rolled out with this good pussy bitch. It was a damn good Sunday night.*

"What the fuck?!!"

My heart stopped at the sound of some nigga's voice from behind me. I stopped stroking and my heart stopped beating. This crazy bitch pushing me off and out of her with this scared-ass look on her face really made me sweat bullets.

My dick went limp as a bitch.

I jumped to my feet and turned around just in time to catch a nasty left hook to my chin. "Damn," I swore, winc-

ing and working my jaw as I bent low and barreled toward that fool. I sent him flying back against the wall.

"Oh shit," Big Butt Belinda swore before she let out a high-pitched scream that made me want to slap her silly.

He bent over my body and delivered hard-ass blows to my back as I put some serious work to his side. Shit crashed from the walls onto the floor as we scuffled and fought like two pit bulls. It was winner take all in that motherfucker.

When another of his hooks sent me stumbling back I shook it off and rushed back toward him to lift his ass like a little bitch. Belinda let out another high-pitched scream when I flung that fool in the corner with a big-ass THUD. He slumped down to the floor like a puppet.

'Bout sick of this shit, I turned and charged over to lift the edge of the bed where I had slid my nine. I grabbed it and the upper hand. That cold steel felt good in my hand. It felt like power. Control. Fuck the dumb shit.

I pointed the gun at his chest as he struggled to his feet. "Sit down, bitch," I told him coldly, sounding like I felt the power and enjoyed the control. Truth? I was scared as hell. I know better than to pull a gun unless I was ready to use it. Was I ready to kill this nigga? Nah, her pussy wasn't that serious.

I looked in his eyes and even though he couldn't see it I was just as scared as he looked. For some reason his fear made me a little cockier. Bolder.

"Come here, Betty—"

"Belinda," she corrected me with attitude from her spot on the bed.

"What . . . the . . . fuck . . . ever," I told her with my eyes still locked on this nigga. Who was he? Her man? Her overprotective brother? Her pimp? What the fuck?

At this point it didn't even matter.

"Bitch, get the fuck over here," I barked, feeling that power and control again.

She came into my line of vision with that dingy flowered sheet still wrapped around that banging-ass body that drew my attention as she skated circles around me. Bee to honey, baby, bee to honey. "Drop the sheet," I told her with as much steel in my voice as I held in my hand.

I didn't have to look at her to know she hesitated. Pretty sure she didn't have to look at me to know I wasn't playing either. "Now," I told her.

Even as I felt the breeze and heard the rustle of the sheet falling to the floor I didn't take my eyes off of homeboy. I wanted to humiliate him. I wanted to punish him for putting his hands on me.

"Suck my dick," I ordered her, keeping my gun steady on him.

I could tell he wanted to say something, but he didn't. Not once. Not even when I felt her trembling body squat down to take my dick in her mouth . . .

That was a crazy fucking night. I guess it didn't help a damn thing that I knocked his ass upside the head with the gun after she swallowed the last of my cum like her ass was hungry.

As I look up into his face I had a feeling this night is going to be even crazier. Even under the dark of night I can see this Negro want some of me. "Well, motherfucker, if you want some come and get some. Fuck that."

That fool races around the car and reaches in to start swinging. The pain is wicked crazy and I take a chance to look up just in time to see him hit me across the forehead with a small pipe. I close my fingers around my piece sitting under my seat and I sit up straight to push my weight against the door. It hits his ass hard as hell, knocking him back from my ride just long enough for me to raise my gun and fire.

His body jerks as each bullet tears into his body.

POW!

POW!

POW!

He falls backward onto the cold and hard street. My heart pounds like a motherfucker. I shot that motherfucker. Oh shit. Oh shit. What the fuck.

Shaterica brought me this nine from a pawnshop last Christmas. It didn't take me long to talk her into it. I carried the gun but I never shot this motherfucker. Never. I ain't no killer. I ain't no banger. I sell knockoff Gucci bags and shit like that. Women are my specialty. Not this shit. Not death.

I feel sick as hell.

Is he dead?

Did I kill him?

Oh shit.

I look up and down the empty street. If anybody had been lurking outside in this heat, gunshots had a way of makin' motherfuckers scatter.

I hop out my car and stand over his body. His blood is already pooling the street. My eyes get big as shit when he sits up and tries to get to his feet. What the fuck?

Like on auto pilot I raise the gun and fire again.

POW!

The bullet enters his head, sending his body back down onto the bloody street.

I got to get the fuck outta here. I race back into my car and squeal away. My eyes look at his body in the sideview mirror.

I killed that nigga. I killed that nigga. Oh shit. I couldn't remember his name. I couldn't even remember his name and I killed him. I killed somebody. I killed Reggie . . . no . . . Ricky . . . no . . . no . . . it's Red. That nigga's name is—*was*—Red. He was Big Butt Belinda's man and we been beefin' ever since that crazy-ass night.

I have to grip the steering wheel tighter 'cause my palms are sweating like crazy. My heart feels like it's gonna bust out my chest. I wouldn't be surprised if I didn't shit up my damn self 'cause for sure I got the bubble guts.

What if somebody called the police when they heard the shots? What if somebody was lookin' out the window and saw me or the car? What the fuck am I gonna do? I can't go to jail. I *ain't* going to jail. Fuck that.

That nigga hit me first. He walked up to my ride with

a damn pipe and I just defended myself. Uhn-uhn. I ain't stupid. That shit ain't even gone to work for a black man in Georgia. A black man in Georgia carrying a gun registered to his girl. Shit.

As I tear up the streets with my wheels I keep hearing the shots in my head. *Pow! Pow! Pow! Pow!*

One gun. Four bullets. One dead man.

Jail. Punk motherfuckers looking for *any* hole to fuck. Becoming somebody's bitch. The death penalty.

I feel even sicker.

I glance down at the gun lying on the leather passenger seat. *Think, Rhak. Think.*

I need a plan.

I need help.

I need to get the fuck out of this shit by *any* means fucking necessary.

4

The Pimp

"I got something better than money," Momma says, removing a pack of cigarettes from the pocket of her robe and lighting up.

I laugh. "Ain't shit better than money," I say and head toward the kitchen to peep out the refrigerator. I know she tends to forget to eat.

"One of your old tricks came by to see me today," she singsongs like an *American Idol* reject.

"I don't have time to play 'Guess the Ho,' Momma," I say, popping open the fridge. The only thing staring back at me is a bright-ass lightbulb and a yellow box of Arm and Hammer. My shoulders deflate. This shit is getting real old.

"I've been meaning to go to the grocery store," she says, trying to cut off my speech before I get started. The thing is I know she makes plenty of money to have food up in this motherfucker. I just pray her ass isn't sucking on that glass dick again. Trust when I say it's a miracle when someone kicks the pipe once; I doubt she'll have the strength to do it again.

But ever since this disease . . .

I slam the door and turn on her, but at the last second I decide to save my breath. "Fuck it. Just write me a list. I'll hire someone to take care of this shit."

A lopsided grin spreads across her face. "You still have a soft spot for your momma, don't you?"

She walks up to me and cups the sides of my face like she used to do whenever I brought home my report card loaded with As. Don't get it twisted. I'm a smart nigga—always have been.

Instead of answering, I lean forward and plant a kiss on the center of her forehead. "Don't get too sentimental. I'm taking it out of your cut."

She laughs.

Truth be told, I'm the only child who comes and sees about her. My fast-ass sisters act like they forgot the way to Bentley Manor. They're too busy letting rappers slide credit cards down the crack of their asses to see about their own damn momma.

"When I get you this food, don't let me hear that you've been selling it out on the streets like Smokey's crazy ass used to do."

"Smokey was a damn junkie. I ain't no damn junkie," Momma spats, sucking on a cancer stick. Her denial was about as thick as the cloud of smoke floating around her.

I shake my head thinking about Bentley Manor's old numero uno crackhead who used to walk the streets selling his own kids' toys and God knows what else just to get a hit. It's a damn shame. I remember the days when Smokey was a star athlete and shit. He thought he was going to roll up out of here on hoop dreams. But reality is a motherfucker when you ain't got a plan B. I ain't a bit surprised he blew his damn brains out. Hell, if I still lived in Bentley Manor I probably would've done the same thing myself.

This place has a way of weighing down on a person. It creeps into your bones and settles into your soul. Hell, a lot of these motherfuckers look like the walking dead to me. That includes those two old bitches, sitting out on their stoop gossiping about people's business.

Fuck them. They're just two miserable bitches because they're trapped in this hellhole. At least I got out.

I take a good look around; a lot of times I wonder how the fuck my momma raised five kids in this cramped motherfucker. That's the beauty of a single mom; they often make a way out of no way. At least when my pussy empire took off, I was able to lace the place up with top of the line furniture and high-tech gadgets. Her place looked like bullshit on the outside but it was blinged the fuck out. It was the least I could do, since she fucked up the house I'd bought her a few years back. She'd turned the motherfucker into a damn crackhouse and the Home Owners Association ran her out of the neighborhood. Goes to show that sometimes you can take a ho out of the hood, but you can't take the hood out of the ho.

Momma tried to live with me and Renee, but they mix about as well as oil and water and before I knew it Momma ran back to Bentley Manor, determined to keep her independence.

I glance at my watch, wanting to speed this shit along before the walls start to cave in on me. "C'mon. I got to head down to the club and handle some business."

"I told you, sweet. I got something better than money."

"Momma, what kind of crazy shit are you talking about now?"

"One of your old tricks dropped off a package for you."

I already don't like the sound of that bullshit. I step back and lean on my pimp stick in preparation for whatever bad news she's about to slap on me. "What trick and what sort of package?"

One side of Momma's lips quirk up—another indication I ain't gonna like what she was about to unload.

"Corrine, get out here!"

I frown. "Who the fuck is Corrine?"

I hear a door open down the short hallway and look up to see who momma had in the apartment while she was servicing a john. I swear nothing stops my momma's flow.

Once I forced her into retirement and she just started fucking everything for free and said when you find a job you enjoy then it doesn't feel like work.

Hell, what can I say to that?

Momma's package finally stepped into the living room.

The last thing I expected was to see some fresh-face Cosby kid look-alike who looked like she'd spent the last hour looking for a lost puppy.

I know Momma isn't trying to outpimp a pimp. "She's a bit young to be working for me, don't you think?" I walk over to the girl and checked her out. My guess is she's fourteen knocking on fifteen with long skinny legs, narrow hips and a chest that was still MIA. "Who on earth trusted you to babysit someone?" I ask, laughing.

"Some trick named Chocolate Angel."

The name is like a punch in the gut. Images of the most luscious pole rider I've ever known bubble to the front of my brain that I almost get a hard-on in front of my own damn momma.

"I take it you remember her?"

I clear my throat and eyeball the kid again. This time, I take in the soft, full mouth, the almost straight nose, and cinnamon-colored eyes. The girl has my eyes. "Oh, shit."

The girl folds her arms as she takes her time checking me out.

"And I take it that you finally see the family resemblance?" Momma says.

"She's not . . ."

"Chocolate Angel says she is. Had a birth certificate and everything." She reached into the front of her robe and pulled out a folded piece of paper.

Hell, I don't even want to look at it and, frankly, I don't need to. Instead, we just continue to stare each other down. Let me tell you, I'm more than impressed that mini-me meets my gaze as bold as you please. This let me know that her whole innocent look meant one thing: Trouble.

"Renee is going to hit the roof."

Momma cackles. "You got that shit right."

All plans to run by the club were tossed aside. I had a much bigger problem on my hands: telling my wife that we now have a teenage daughter to raise.

A fucking daughter.

Now how in the hell is a pimp supposed to raise a damn girl? Chocolate Angel, or rather Tracy, was wrong for this shit right here.

I lean forward and glance around Destiny to steal another peek at my own flesh and blood, marveling over a miracle, because about thirteen years back I had a little cut and snip to prevent this very thing. Hell, Renee couldn't have any kids and she knew my ass was a fuckaholic. So to prevent my ass from slipping up and getting another bitch pregnant, we agreed I'd get fixed and put to rest her wild ideas that I would eventually leave her ass to play house with some trick.

Now here I come bringing home a fifteen-year-old daughter.

Shit is definitely about to hit the fan now.

Destiny slides a hand into my lap, just a reassuring caress, I'm sure, until her long hands roam toward my crotch.

"Not now, baby," I mutter, easing back in my seat. My temples are already banging like a drum.

"Whateva," Destiny mumbles, rolling her eyes.

Corrine shifts in her seat so she can get a better look at Destiny, who's sitting between us.

"So are you a man or what?" she asks, her face twisting in disgust. Her voice is a bit high—almost Rosie Perez–like.

Destiny puts on her best smile and says, "I guess I'm a 'or what'," she answers. "You got a problem with that, Little Miss Sunshine?"

Corrine's eyes shift to mine. "So what? You two faggots or some shit like that?"

Whatever goodwill I had toward this stranger/child just went the fuck out the window.

"Who the fuck is she calling a faggot?" Destiny swivels her neck toward me. "Daughter or not. You better check this bitch before I wreck this bitch."

One warning glare from me and Destiny shuts that shit down, but her anger radiates throughout the car like a son of a bitch. I return my attention to Corrine and she again looks unfazed by coming within a hairsbreadth of getting her ass whupped by an angry trannie more than twice her size.

Impressive and disturbing.

"Let's get one thing straight, Corrine," I say in my most patient voice. "Blood you might be, but it doesn't mean your ass can't sleep on the street." I hit her with another leveled gaze so she can see I mean that shit. "Right now kicking you to the curb is an option I'm warming up to."

For the first time uncertainty creeps into her eyes.

"Watch your mouth and save your ass," I say, and return my attention to the passing scenery outside my window. I already know I'm not down for this fatherhood shit.

My new crib is this fly-as-fuck mansion out in Alpharetta—one of the many affluent suburbs of Atlanta. It used to belong to Junior's NFL superstar cousin, Tyrik Jefferson—that is, until his ass was arrested for killing his pregnant girlfriend about a year back. His loss is my motherfuckin' gain.

After the Bentley rolls to a stop and I wait for Anderson to come and open my door I'm thinking of all the things I can say to jump off this conversation with Renee. Nothing comes to mind to buffer this storm I'm about to go through so I might as well get this motherfucker over with.

Once we step out of the ride and into the house, I instruct Destiny to take Corrine to the kitchen and find her something to eat. Lord knows she didn't get shit at my mom's crib.

"I don't babysit," Destiny says, cradling her hands on her hips and giving me more attitude that I just flat-out don't need right now.

"You do whatever the fuck I tell you to do," I snap.

Destiny's eyes bug the fuck out because I rarely lose my cool with her, but I'll coldcock her like the man she is before I let her disrespect me and she knows it.

"Fine," she hisses through her teeth and turns on her ridiculously high heels. "Bring your ass on, Little Miss Sunshine." She stomps her way toward the kitchen.

Corrine's confidence is dwindling by the second and she flashes an uncertain look my way before she follows Destiny to the kitchen.

I, on the other hand, stroll off in the opposite direction; across the marbled foyer, through the expansive living room, and up a private back staircase for the short cut to the master bedroom. I enter the room just in time to see Renee sliding open her pussy's thick lips to reveal her glistening pink pearl.

I freeze with an instant hard-on, my mouth watering.

Renee meets my eye with a wicked smile and reaches over to the nightstand to whip out a thick, twelve-inch, clear-colored vibrator. She turns it on and the shaft starts twirling columns of rotating beads. My baby's hips roll in anticipation while she first dips the thick shaft into her mouth. She closes her eyes as if imagining the large toy as being the real thing. She gives the vibrating shaft a few good slurps before attempting to ease more inches into her mouth until the damn thing had to be rammed against her tonsils.

It's a damn sexy sight. Her bright candy-apple red painted lips, honey-golden skin, and naturally thick sandy-brown hair cascading curls across our black silk pillows. Hell, I want to fuck now and talk later.

Expertly, Renee glides the vibrator out of her hot mouth and places the now wet shaft against her hard, dusty brown nipples. She only emits a small moan before forming a wet trail down the center of her curvy body and then into her juicy wet pussy.

At first it's just the tip and then she pulls it out and slides some of her thick glistening juices over her clit. Her husky moan has a way of sounding like a purring cat.

She knows I love that shit.

Greedily, she plunges the vibrator back into her sopping wet pussy. The sound of the whirling beads becomes a deep muffle. She pumps the fake cock; her pussy widens and starts talking back—nasty talk-smacking, gurgling, and whatnot. Renee swirls her hips, sliding more inches deep inside her. It's a fucking amazing sight to watch her body swallow damn near eleven inches and even more amazing to watch the pleasure that explodes across her face.

"Oh, shit," she coos and then sucks air in between her clenched teeth. "Oh. Fuck. I'm. Cuuuummming!"

There's no mistaking when my baby girl cums. My baby is a squirter. Hot syrupy clear cum shoots off all over her play toy and drips down in between her thighs. Her hips are swirling like a tornado and amazingly she takes in a few more inches on her vibrator, which now sounds as if it's drowning.

Delilah, another one of my working girls, approaches the bed and smiles down at my wife. She lightly plays with the diamond stud pierced through Renee's right nipple before bending down and taking it into her mouth. She gives it a few playful nibbles while drifting one hand down between her legs and slowly pulling out the long fake cock planted between Renee's legs. To show how much a freak she is, Delilah takes the dripping wet cock and slides it between her pink frosted lips for a taste.

"And cut," the director shouts, and then removes the hand of the girl who has been steadily jerking him off during shooting. "Everyone take ten."

The small production team encircling the bed begins clapping. A few even whistle. But all of us have hard-ons strong enough to cut steel.

Flashing her small fan club a bright smile, Renee climbs out of bed and pulls on a see-through, white lace robe and heads in my direction.

"How'd I do, sweet?" she asks, leaning up on her toes to lay a kiss on me.

I can't help but fill my hands with her plump golden-onion booty for a good squeeze and rub my dick up against her sopping wet monkey. The way we get down, it would have been nothing for me to fuck her right here in front of the whole crew, but I have other pressing matters on my plate right now.

"I need to holla at you for a minute," I tell her, needing to stick to business.

She stiffens and pulls back to meet my eye. "Sounds serious." For the most part, Renee is what is typically described as a ride-or-die chick. When she's down with someone, she is all the way the fuck down. But it doesn't mean that she doesn't have her hot-button issues that can turn a pimp's happy home into pure hell.

Before I can open my mouth, Renee's eyes sweep around me and her face immediate crunches up. "Who the fuck is she?"

I turn around and see Corrine standing in the hall, her eyes big as fuck. "I thought I told your ass to stay in the kitchen."

Corrine backs up, looking like I just slapped the shit out of her.

"Get the fuck on," I snap, since she seems to be hard of hearing.

She takes off then. Shit. I've been a father all of one hour and my "daughter" has met her ho grandmother, her father's transvestite lover, and her pornstar stepmother. I'm sure to win father of the year with this bullshit.

"Tavon," Renee says and successfully draws my attention back to her. All playfulness has vanished from her eyes.

"Who is that little bitch and why the fuck does she look like you?"

5

The Killer

For ten years I've been rotting in this cage, convinced that I was in the bowels of hell. When I was first locked down, I felt and was treated like an animal. I strolled up in here with my fingers in the air and screaming *"FUCK YOU!"* to the world.

Welcomed by my fellow Disciples also on lockdown, a nigga like me just thought he was home.

Nigga.

That's how I used to view myself—how a lot of my black brothas view themselves. Once upon a time the white man enslaved us with that word and now we willingly do it to ourselves.

Damn shame.

Sitting up on the edge of my cot in the hell Georgia calls Jesup Federal Correctional Institute, a good thirty minutes before the morning wake-up call, I can't believe this day has finally come. 'Course I haven't served nowhere near the amount of time I should. I've put to sleep a few brothas the state hasn't prosecuted me for, twelve, to be exact, but I'm not the confessing type—despite my finding the road to Allah.

What can I say? Once an animal gets locked down, he has only two choices: prepare for hell or crawl in the opposite direction. I've crawled and now I'm ready to stand. I won't lie and say I'm not worried about the temptation of the street, the lure of the hustle when I leave this place. In fact, that's all I worry about, since I'm leaving today.

Early release for good behavior. Now tell me that's not a sign. I'm being given another chance and this time I'm going to walk the straight and narrow and be true to my girl Zoey.

I glance up to her picture on the wall, and can feel a smile ease around my thick lips. Zoey and I go way back. I was her first and only. We hooked up in the eighth grade when she used to hang out at my man M. Dawg's crib. I peeped her out because she curved in all the right places and knew all the words to World Famous Supreme's "Hey DJ." She tried to hold out, keep her legs closed. But after three weeks I hit a home run and rocked her world.

After that, there wasn't a damn thing she wouldn't do for me. Make a few drop-offs, get rid of a hot piece, or lie her ass off about where her man was at the time of his latest crime. I loved her for that shit.

I just didn't know it.

I might have been Zoey's one and only, but at the time she was just one of many—too many. I knocked up one chick and now have a twelve-year-old son running around. I used women like I used drugs. They were just a temporary fix to a deeply rooted problem. Problems I denied having.

Her love scared the shit out of me. Parts of me kept hoping she'd wake up and see I wasn't worth the pain. So I cheated, lied, used, and abused.

And still she remained by my side—tears and all.

So twelve murders, thirty-two robberies, countless aggravated assaults, and moving some heavy weight in and out of Bentley Manor later, here I am.

I'm here because of a combination of those things, all except the murders, of course. Georgia's three strikes law did what nothing else could do: it woke my ignorant ass up.

Sometimes I can hear the devil laughing, telling me that he owns my ass and that I'm not fooling anyone. Those are the times I fall back on my knees and pray for hours. Only time will tell whether it's enough.

For most of my thug life and gangsta ways, I was young, dumb, and didn't know any better. I could do like some of my brothers and blame my bad choices on whitey—big brother and the like but the truth of the matter is that it was my black brothas, the Disciples, who put the gun in my hand, taught me how to aim, shoot, rob, steal, rape, and get high.

But in order to get in, I had to prove I was down. Let them know that I wasn't scared and was ready to be a man—or what I thought defined being a man. So at fourteen I made my first kill.

A boy in my own neighborhood.

A random boy who happened to be on the wrong corner at the wrong time.

Kadrian Johnson.

The name is permanently burned into my head as well as the sight of him spinning around when my bullet hit his shoulder and then lifting off the ground when my second bullet hit his chest. He was dead before he slammed into the concrete. I learned later he was just fifteen. He and his family lived in the same hellhole I called home: Bentley Manor.

Not only that, he looked like me. A lot like me.

When I replay that night, my mind plays tricks and shows me shooting myself. That shit fucks with me.

But I did it all for the same reasons that anyone does anything: love and acceptance. I grew up without a damn thing. Bentley Manor provided a roof, but my father left skid marks after making his sperm deposit and my momma, just fourteen years older than me, didn't know nothing about raising a baby and dropped my ass in a Dumpster in the back of a Circle K gas station.

There have been plenty of nights when I've thought the world would have been better off if I had died in that muthafucka.

At least there would be a few more people still walking around today if I had. But once I get out of here, no one is going to call Demarcus Jones a fuckup anymore.

That's a promise.

"Rise and shine, assholes!" Charlie, the prison guard on my block, shouts and starts banging on the prison bars like a BeBe kid on a red Kool-Aid sugar high. Everybody on the block hates his guts, mainly because the only difference between us and him is that he wears a uniform.

Charlie controls everything from drugs to sex on the block. If you need anything from him, it's going to cost you—usually some ass pussy. But I don't get down like that.

Period.

When Charlie reaches my cell, he stops banging on the iron cage to sneer. "Well, Big Preacher Man. I hear today is your day."

I can't help but crack a smile. That's more than he usually gets out of me. Over the years we've clashed more than a few times. At six-two, he was blacker than coal and was as hard and tough as a walking brick building. In an ugly contest, I can't think of a single soul who could beat him.

At six-four, 235 pounds of raw muscles, I don't need a gun to put nobody's ass to sleep. That was the old me. Now folks around here just call me Big Preacher Man. Mainly because that's all I do nowadays.

Some laugh me off, some fake the funk, trying to psych

out the parole board, and others, like me, are just downright desperate for answers.

Back then I couldn't understand how black folks could so readily accept the white man's God. For hundreds of years they had used the Holy Bible as the means to justify the enslavement of a whole race of people while killing off another.

That was just my ignorance talking.

Now I see a lot of similarities in the Christian and Muslim faiths. The devil is in the details. It's his weapon to keep brothers like me confused and in the dark. Growing up in Bentley Manor with a foster mother only interested in the government check that came along with me, I had no real concept of what love truly was. I thought it was the acceptance and brotherhood offered to me on the streets.

I would've died for those brothers and they would have done the same for me.

Charlie's sneer deepens. "Boys and I got a pool going on you," he says. Despite my not showing the least bit of interest, he continues. "See, I think you'll be back in here in five months. Pete says a year and Big Earl has actually bought into your Holy Roller bullshit."

What was left of my smile melts off my face.

He laughs. "What? You think I don't know bullshit when I smell it?"

He leans in and draws in a good strong whiff. "Ah, yeah. Freshly churned manure. That's the kind of stench you can't wash off."

The image of that old Dumpster behind the gas station leaps to the front of my mind. The devil trying to convince me what Charlie is saying is true. There are some things you can't wash off.

Instead of letting him bait me, I find my smile again. "Sorry, Charlie, but you're going to lose this one." I pick up my Quran and hold it up for him. "I'm a changed man."

"Four months," he amends, laughs, and walks off to bang on the next line of bars.

As the morning rolls on, I'm surprised Charlie's words stay with me as well as his awful cackle. Around noon while I'm being processed for release, I catch sight of him again and he holds up four fingers and jiggles his eyebrows.

I shake my head. He has me all wrong.

An hour later, I'm finally handed my walking papers as well as the name and address of my new parole officer. Call me crazy, but when I walk out I swear the air smells fresher, tastes cleaner.

However, the best part is seeing my baby, Zoey, climb out of a silver Toyota. She's a thicker woman now. Her curves wider, her thighs and breasts larger, but her smile with the two raisin-sized dimples is still the same. While she runs toward me in a pair of tight jeans and a cloud-white, long T, I swear she's the most beautiful woman in the world.

"Demarcus!" she shouts, leaping in the air, her legs

wrapping around my waist. I catch her with no problem, her warm body a welcome weight in my arms. "Oh, God, baby. I can't believe this day is finally here." She showers kisses all over my face. The few that land on my lips are like candy that melts in your mouth.

"I love you. I love you. I love you."

"I love you, too," I say and mean it. The fact that she's here is amazing, since it was my attempt to kill her that landed me in the joint in the first place.

6

The Playa

I used to talk mad shit about broke-down, busted, and disgusted Bentley Manor. I done seen some crazy shit go down in this motherfucker since I moved in with my girl a couple of months ago. But anytime you cram too many motherfuckers in one spot, you gone have shit poppin' all day, every damn day. Shit, most of my other bitches either rented houses or stayed out in the boondocks in trailers. But right when I think of givin' up this crappy motherfucker to sit up in a jail, I'm lovin' Bentley Manor like a motherfucker.

I reach up with shaky hands as I feel sweat run down the side of my face. It's hot up in this brick motherfucker. And them bullshit-ass box fans we got ain't doin' shit but drawin' in more of that muggy-ass Georgia heat. Right now my balls sticky as hell.

I take another drag off my blunt as I watch through

the dirty fingerprints on the window at bad-ass kids runnin' around enjoyin' their summer vacation. Shaterica be talkin' about having kids and shit. Say she want a baby boy that looks just as good as me. I can't blame her but I damn sure can ignore her ass. The last thing I want is a child right now. I got to do me, and the white man cuttin' into my funds on the regular is a fuckin' problem. A major problem.

Through the smoke comin' up around my face I watch this head named Delia wanderin' around the parkin' lot with her eyes fixed on the ground. Bitch probably lookin' for change or hopin' to run across some money to help buy a hit.

Back in the day, before that crack hit her ass hard I knew Delia from Hollywood Court projects. She was a badass bitch back then. Tall, red, ridiculous body, dressed to kill with a face that looked like it ain't belong nowhere in *this* hood. I tried to holla at her and she made me feel like shit on her shoe. Well, payback is a no good son of a bitch. Went from Miss High and Mighty to a two-dollar crack whore. Ain't life a bitch? *Humph,* now anytime I get two dollars—and I mean no more than two—I sneak my ass away from Shaterica and pay that mixed bitch them same measly-ass two dollars to suck my dick. And I mean nasty, too. Swallow up all my nut and lick it clean, too. The bitch works hard for the money.

I feel my dick getting warm in my baggy jeans and I'm just about to go hit Shaterica's money stash for two bucks when I see my girl's Honda turn through the damn near tore-down wrought-iron gates. *Just the bitch I been waitin' on.*

Killin' that motherfucker last night had me tense as a bitch and I can go for a Delia special for real. It'll wait though. That crackhead bitch ain't going nowhere . . . and neither am I. Bentley Manor is home . . . for now.

I bite the tip of my blunt and watch Shaterica climb out of her car. Do I feel any guilt for what I'm about to do? No. Life is what it is and I gotta do what I gotta do. Fuck it. A nigga like me ain't goin' to jail and I *mean* that shit.

I fucked up killin' that motherfucker in the street like that. Right now the police could be out lookin' for a black Honda. They might even have the tag. All of this could lead right back to me.

Sorry. I'm not goin' be able to do it.

Right now, I need her more than I ever needed any woman. I watch her like a hawk as she parks in front of our building and climbs her big ass out the car.

Don't get me wrong, Shaterica is finer than a mother-fucker with that good hair, sweet caramel complexion, big eyes that can make a dude's knees go weak, and those Angie Stone lips that are made to kiss or to suck a dick. But it's below her neck that it all goes the fuck down-hill. She makes up two Angie Stones *and* a Mo'nique. The pussy good. Shit, the pussy is damn good, but Shateri-ca's a big bitch and it's some major exercise to get to that motherfucker. For real.

She walks around the car and waves to someone across the courtyard. My eyes shift in that direction. I ain't surprised to see them two old ladies sittin' they nosy ass in their usual spots by their buildings. They ain't shit but a couple of fuckin' spoons, always dippin' in people business and shit when they old ass should be feelin' bad that they gone die in the projects. Over a hundred years between the both of them and they ass ain't made it no further than the front door of their damn buildings.

Fuck 'em.

My eyes shift again and I see Delia headed behind the building across from me with one of Kaseem's foot soldiers. One good blow for another. *Dumb bitch.*

While I wait on my girl to waddle her ass up them two flight of stairs to the apartment, I turn away from the window and kick off my jeans and boxers. My oversized Rocawear white T-shirt goes flying on one of the many piles of dirty clothes on the floor. I lay back on the squeaky full-sized bed that is as square and flat as a big-ass box of cereal. Last, but not least, I jerk my hip to the side to make that long, thick dick of mine lay across my thigh like a snake.

See, I know Shaterica. I been inside of her life, her pussy, her apartment, but most important her motherfuckin' head. And trust that there ain't much goin' on inside that motherfucker. This bitch loves me *and* this big dick of mine. And once I lay the right words and the right dickin' down on her dumb ass, she will do exactly what I want her to do. She better.

The thin-ass fake wooden door of the bedroom swings open and she strolls in, turnin' sideways to walk in the room.

"Damn, I missed you, baby," I tell her, reachin' out for her with my arms spread wide and already knowin' she's comin' straight to me.

"I missed you too," she says, sitting her fake Gucci purse on the bed as she looks around the room. "But why you ain't clean up? I worked hard all night long and I don't like my room lookin' like this, Rhakmon."

This bitch act like this the motherfuckin' Ritz. More like The Shitz. I start to flip on her ass but I got bigger fish to fry than an argument about some dirty-ass bedroom. "Baby, when I tell you the trouble my ass in you gonna forget 'bout this dirty room just like I did."

She looks concerned and shit. "What's goin' on?" she asks me, her southern girl accent thick as hell.

I drop my head in my hands and I don't look up until tears are in my eyes. "I . . . I . . . shot this guy last night—"

"What?"

For a hot second I think I lost her when she steps back from me and puts one of her pudgy hands over her mouth. Fuck that, I need this big bitch, so I cry like when I was eight and my grandmother, Mom-Mom, was about to whup my ass with a switch. Snot runnin'. Shoulders shakin'. Chest heavin'. Eyes red like a motherfucker.

Seconds later I feel her hands on my shoulders pullin'

me back toward her soft-ass body. "Talk to me, Rhak. Tell me what's goin' on, baby."

"I didn't mean to do . . . do it," I tell her as I turn on the edge of the bed and press my face against her big old titties. "He tried to carjack me last night—"

"Last night? In my car?"

I nod and I don't look up because I don't want her to see I'm lyin' my ass off. "Before you went to work."

She leans back from me and I lean into her, not lettin' her get the fuck away. I need her. I need her bad as hell. "Did someone see you shoot him?" she asks.

I know her. I really know her. I make it my job to know the ins and outs of every bitch I fuck with so that I know just how far to push them for what I want.

"I don't know, baby."

She presses my head closer to her chest and one of her nipples is hard and poking through her orange T-shirt. I ain't gone lie. I had to fight the urge to reach out with my mouth and suck that motherfucker. Big titties is big titties and Shaterica had a set of 50s made to suck.

I wrap my arms around her wide-ass waist and hug her body close to mine. "I already got two assaults charges on my record and if I get caught my ass might get a murder charge. That's fuckin' life or the death penalty or some shit, Sha. What the fuck I'm gone do?"

Her hands are rubbing circles on my back. Takin' care of a nigga. "But you said he tried to carjack you, so ain't that self-defense?"

I look at her like she crazy. "For a black man in Georgia?"

"I know, baby. I know."

"This shit fucks up everythin' when they catch me, Sha." I drop my head in my hands again. "How the fuck we gone get married and have a baby if my ass locked up behind some dumb shit."

And that's when my body gets still as hell because I just dropped the kicker. The deal breaker. The motherfuckin' showstopper.

"Get married? Have a baby?"

Her big body is shakin'—fuckin' shakin'—and shit. Women are so fuckin' easy to play.

Before I look up at her, I make sure my face is sadder than a motherfucker. "Damn right, Shaterica. I love you, girl. This was supposed to be our year. Just when everythin' is goin' our way here come this bullshit."

I look deep into her eyes and I see all I want to see. The trust. The love. The devotion. The desire to help a nigga out.

"If I get locked up I'm gonna die or get life and then me and you ain't gone never be." Fuck it, pushin' that shit home once more 'gain ain't gone hurt a damn thing.

She drops her head on top of mine and I feel her tears wet my cheek as she cries. "I can't live without you, Rhakmon. Fuck that. I ain't gone live without you."

Bingo.

"What can I do, baby? Just tell me and I'll do anything for you. Fuck the dumb shit."

See, she works at night and a nigga like me had all night to get this shit together for her ass bright and early this mornin' when she got off work. Still, I hoped and wished like a motherfucker but who knew if it would work.

"Unless . . ."

"Unless what?" she asks, jumpin' right on it.

"Naw, I couldn't ask you to do that for me."

Shaterica puts her hand on my chin and pulls my face up so that I am lookin' into her eyes again. "It ain't for me. It's for us. Tell me what I gotta do for my man and I'm gonna make it do what it do, baby."

"You could say that he tried to jack you and you shot him. Without a record and you're a woman, they'll believe you."

Her face scrunches up. "Wait a min—"

"This way we can be married this year and get the fuck up outta this ratty motherfucking projects . . . together."

"Together?" she asks sounding like a six-year-old child and not a grown-ass woman.

I stand up and press my face into her neck as I grind my dick against the softness of her belly. Like I said, the pussy good as a motherfucker and my dick gets hard as the jail time I'm duckin' like a motherfucker. My hands massage her ass as I suck her neck. When I feel her body shiver and her hands come down to grab my ass like it's goin' somewhere, I know this dickin' down is just the last push I need to get her ass down to the police station. Oh,

I'm gone fuck this bitch like I ain't never fucked any bitch in my life.

Peep this—and don't hate the playa—but I just talked this girl into takin' a murder charge for me. Oh, I'm a bad boy. For real.

7

The Dealer

The last thing I am is a stereotype. I completely blow this jacked-up vision of what a drug dealer is supposed to be. I don't walk around carrying guns and shit. My trunk is filled with shopping bags, not concealed weapons. My ass ain't angry. I'm not stupid as fuck—I even have my associates degree in Computer Technology. I've never ordered nobody killed and don't plan on it. I don't even smoke weed and I hardly ever drink. The last thing I am is a 2008 version of Nino Brown. I don't want to do shit but make my money, dress my ass off, get bitches, do good by my people, and have fun. Fuck it.

The thing is, it ain't just the people out of the hood that got that hyped-up version of what the fuck I'm supposed to say and do. Now, don't get me wrong, my ass ain't soft worth a damn but I'm no Maleek. That motherfucker would choke a fool out over fifty damn dollars.

My boys want me to be the same way.

From where I'm leaning against the rear of my milk-white Cadillac, I cut my eyes over to the corner at the sound of someone hollering out in pain. Okay, not someone. I know exactly who the fuck it is and I know exactly why that cat gettin' his ass beat by Usher. Lloyd got caught with his hand in the cookie jar big-time. Since Usher caught him, Usher is making it his personal project to punish him.

I wince as Usher delivers a fisted blow that lands against Lloyd's dark jaw. A sound like ice being crushed echoes and my stomach turns as blood gushes from his mouth.

Being in some deserted parking lot late at night whuppin' some fool's ass until he's bloody isn't my type of fucking party. "That's enough," I call over to Usher just as Lloyd's body slumps to his knees and his head lags back.

Usher delivers another slap against his bloodied cheek. *WHAP!*

I push off the car to rise to my sneakered feet. "I said that's enough," I stress, my voice hard. I demand to be heard when I speak. I never forget my position. My Air Force 1s eat up the space between me and them. I reach them in just enough time to catch Usher's fist before it lands another blow.

He swings his head to look at me. His eyes are red with rage and his chest is heaving like some fucking bull or some shit. His mouth is curled in disgust. Sweat's popping off this motherfucker's head like crazy.

What the fuck? Usher look like a black-ass devil. Evil as fuck. He lookin' like he ready to kill a motherfucker.

"What?" he asks, like he confused or some shit.

I look at him long and hard. "That's enough, Usher," I stress to him again. Ain't nobody trying to kill a motherfucker over no dope or sense of fucking honor. Like I said, I ain't no fucking gangsta. *Scarface, Godfather* and *Goodfellas* don't have me fucked up.

He shakes his bald head like he trying to clear his shit as I undo his fingers from being clutched so tight around the front of Lloyd's bloody shirt. I look down at him for the first time and the chicken and waffles I had for lunch start to come back up. I swallow hard as hell hoping I didn't vomit. His lips are so swollen and bloody they look fake. One of his teeth is hanging loose from his gum. His left eye is swollen shut already and the right one is bloodshot. His nose is twisted to the side and there is a deep gash on his chin—probably from the platinum bulldog ring Usher wears on his right hand. Damn. He fucked up.

As soon as he is free, Lloyd scrambles to his feet and finds the strength to run like Kunta Kinte across the parking lot.

"Why the fuck you lettin' him get away?" Usher roars from behind me; his voice sounds as rough as the asphalt we standin' the fuck on.

The white of Lloyd's wifebeater and sneakers gets smaller as he runs for his life. I turn just in time to see the streetlight glint against the steel 9mm in Usher's tight grip. It's pointed in Lloyd's direction.

POW!

Just as the gun fires I jerk his hand up, sending the bullet up into the night air. "Are you fucking crazy?" I yell at him.

"Shit," he swears as Lloyd disappears around an abandoned Pick and Save.

I shove my hands into my linen shorts as I walk away from him. "This what the fuck you brought me here for? This fake-ass gangsta shit?" I ask him in a low voice as I stop and turn back to look at him.

Usher slides his gun back under his shirt before he uses one large hand to wipe the sweat from his face. "I brought you here so you can man up and handle these motherfuckers. How the hell you gone run these streets and your ass be lettin' niggas handle you any kind of way?"

I just shake my damn head as I look up to the sky. I got enough patience to count every fucking star. "This is about business for me. Plain and simple. Supply and demand."

Usher nods. "I hear what you sayin'. These young fools just be pissin' me off with that thievin' bullshit."

"Don't sweat it," I tell him as I pull my keys out my pocket and walk to my car.

"I'm just used to Maleek's way of doing things," Usher offers as he frowns at the blood staining his dark hand.

"My way or the hard fucking way," we say together.

I don't say shit else as we climb into the car. Even as we eventually ride up Piedmont with my system straight blasting, my thoughts are filled with the bullshit involved in the game—the part of the game that I don't want no part of.

The motherfuckers caught up in the money, power, and respect of pushing the type of weight I deal in.

The wannabe ganstas thinking dope dealing and violence had to go hand in hand.

These bitch-ass niggas looking to take my spot.

Motherfuckers pressing me to handle these streets hard as hell like I'm Gotti or some shit. Motherfuckers better stop taking them rap videos and movies so fucking serious. Any three motherfuckers with the same color shirt calling themselves a gang and out there killing people to prove it.

Always being on my toes to stay the fuck out of jail or at the end of some young buck's damn gun.

Always having to be two steps ahead of everything and every damn body.

I ain't gone lie and say my conscience all fucked up because I'm helping to kill up black people with drugs, because I believe whether I do it or the next man, a junkie gone be a damn junkie. And I ain't one of them motherfuckers handing out dope for free hoping to hook new customers or getting kids to sell for me. I deal with nothing but grown-ass folks who know damn well what the fuck they doing.

Still, I'm tired as hell but as long as my ass in the game I know I got to deal with this shit. I gots to do what the fuck I gots to do. I knew that from the first time I got in where I fit in at fifteen. It's going to stay that way until I get out . . . which is no time soon.

"Maw-Maw," I call out as I close the wooden front door of the house. The scent of something cooking makes my stomach grumble. It reminds me how hungry I am.

The wooden floors and crystal chandelier of the foyer is a long damn way from either my apartment or the dirty tiled floors of Bentley Manor. This is my parents' three-thousand-square-foot home in Alpharetta, Georgia. When they did live in Atlanta it was a long way from spots like Bentley Manor. They weren't rich but my mother's a registered nurse and my father owns a real estate business . . . so they are comfortable as fuck. And my life here in the burbs was comfortable, too. Really, my spoiled ass had no business out in those streets hustling. . . .

"Man, if y'all really want to make some money I can help you out . . . for real."

Usher and I were sitting on his bumpy and beat-down twin bed, looking up at his eighteen-year-old cousin Pee-Wee like he was Biggie or some shit. He was tall, with a fresh fade and enough gold jewelry to open his own store. Every time he moved, his jewelry flashed until my eyes fucking hurt. We were just fifteen. Young as hell and easy to impress. And right then, Pee-Wee was the shit.

From the minute Usher and I sat next to each other in our eighth-grade homeroom class we became the best of friends. It was my first year there and I was glad to have a friend as cool and popular as Usher. For me everything about his life was new and different. I was soaking it all in. The busy-ass three-bedroom apartment where he lived with his mother, three brothers, his aunt, and her four kids. The bunch of people always hanging in the halls or in the front of the project building where they lived. The cars riding by with their systems booming. Random fights between hot girls who would beat and strip each other all at the same time.

There was always something jumping off in the hood and it was different as hell from my life. Different and fun. Different and exciting. Different and addictive. I spent more and more time in Usher's world.

"Y'all look like a couple of hard heads looking for some pussy to spray in," Pee-Wee said, his short and pointy tongue running across his bottom grills as he reached in the pocket of his jeans and pulled out a wad of money.

Our mouths dropped open as he began to count it in our faces.

"Money makes the world go 'round and the drawers go down, young bucks. You understand?"

We nodded like we were in a damn trance or some shit.

Pee-Wee's money fanned out as he gestured with his hands. "I know I'm a ugly motherfucker. Fuck that. I'm like Biggie, keepin' it real, you know?"

He leaned forward and lightly tapped the money against our cheeks. "But this here money makes sure I gets all the pussy I need from all the bitches I need it from. These birds out there today about one thing . . . and this is it."

Fifteen, horny as hell, and tired of jacking my own dick? Pee-Wee's shit was sounding like a damn plan.

"For real?" I asked, ready to get next to something other than my damn hand.

Pee-Wee made a face like "of course." "I paid Georgia twenty dollars to suck my dick in the cafeteria yesterday," he boasted.

Shee-it. My dick got hard right then and there.

"Fine-ass Georgia Wilson with the big ass?" Usher asked.

Pee-Wee nodded like "for sure."

"Where you get all that money from, Pee-Wee?" Usher asked.

Pee-Wee shoved the money back in his pocket and walked over to the banged-up bedroom door to peek out. The constant sounds of the TV and radios blaring mingled with people talking got a little louder than before. As soon as he shut it, it lowered again to a muffle.

He turned and reached under the mattress of the top bunk bed and pulled out a Ziploc of weed. "Smoke it. Sell it. But don't love it. Listen to me and you'll be happier than a moth-erfucker. For real."

Pee-Wee was accidentally shot and killed during a store robbery two years later, but by then me and Usher was selling weed like it was going out of style. Even when my parents moved to Alpharetta and I transferred to another school, I still made my way back to the hood.

During our hustling, I took the lead but we made that money together. We had each other's back. We shopped like crazy, bought enough pussy and bitches to last a life-time, and did whatever we wanted to do because the money was flowing that freely. Shit, it's a whole lotta motherfuck-ers that smoke weed . . . in and out of the hood.

Pushing away my past, I walk down the hall filled with pictures of me and the rest of my family over the years. My ass couldn't help but pause at my framed de-gree in the center of it all. I wonder how proud they would be if they knew how much weed I sold while I was in college. They thought I had a job on campus but my ass wasn't trying to flip no damn burgers or no shit. That bullshit wouldn'ta paid for Ralph, Tommy, Calvin, or shit else.

I follow the sounds of family through the kitchen and out onto the deck. Like every other summer Friday night, my parents, my grandmother Grams, and a few family friends are lounging on the lit deck playing cards while everyone took turns tending to the smoking meat on the grill.

There's a lot about me that my family don't know. They think I work as an accounting clerk for a small law firm. They just met Quilla a few weeks ago and that's because she stressed me the fuck out about it. I even hid that I was locked up in county for four months that time I got caught with a ounce of weed during one of them random traffic stops. To this day they thought I dipped to Virginia with some chick for a hot second.

If I keep it funky right now it's lonely as hell keeping a big part of my damn life from my family, because we're all so close. Still, I know if they ever find out I'm selling drugs they wouldn't fuck with me at all. AT . . . ALL.

I'll have to get this shit straight sooner than later.

8

The Killer

"What? You scared, Demarcus? Is that what the fuck you're telling me?" Terrius Mitchell shouted; spittle flew from his mouth and all over my face.

"Naw, man. I ain't say all that," I answered, hoping my voice don't crack like it usually did when I get nervous.

"Then what the fuck you sayin'?"

My eyes grew wide as I blink up at him. For fourteen I was a small muthafucka praying for a coupla growth spurts.

Terrius glanced around, looking for M. Dawg. "Did you bring this punk mutherfucka here tonight? What the fuck y'all doin' wastin' my time?"

"Nah. Nah. He's cool, man. He's down with The Disciples."

Terrius's lips twitched and his nose flared as if he smelled something foul. "He sure in the hell don't look cool to me."

"*Trust me.*" *M. Dawg glanced at me, silently begging me to pull my shit together.* "*He is.*"

"*Yeah. Yeah. I'm cool,*" *I said, licking my lips and straightening my pencil thin shoulders.*

Fire blazed in Terrius's eyes. "*Then you know what you gotta do.*" *He pressed the gun in my hand.*

I looked down at it, thinking the shit was heavier than I've ever imagined. I licked my lips again and asked, "*Who?*"

"*I don't give a fuck,*" *he spat.* "*Pick somebody. Prove to me your ass is ready to be a man.*"

I don't know why but my eyes began to burn like hell.

"*Is this little piece of shit gonna start crying on me?*" *Terrius roared.*

The menacing group surrounding him snickered and pushed me around.

"*His punk ass ain't gonna do shit,*" *Zeke, the biggest mutherfucka in the group snapped.* "*I say we stomp his ass and teach him a lesson about wastin' our time.*" *He turned his attention to M. Dawg.* "*Him and this pipsqueak muthafucka.*"

M. Dawg's eyes grew wide.

"*I'ma do it,*" *I said, my voice finally cracking.*

More laughter. More shoving.

Though my hand tightened on the gun, it didn't stop trembling.

Terrius smiled down at me, his breath hot against my face, and I'm more convinced than ever that I'm looking into the face of the devil.

"Better not disappoint me, Demarcus."

Right now my options are kill or be killed. I have pestered and worked my way into the inner sanctum of The Disciples and now that I'm here there's no turning back— that's abundantly clear. At that moment, I couldn't remember why I wanted to be a member of one of the most feared underground gangs in Atlanta. What made me think I was tough enough—bad enough—to wear their black-and-white colors?

Hell. On any given night you could find me curled up under my bed crying from another beatdown I'd suffered from my foster mother. She would beat me with whatever was handy. From switches to extension cords, I had so many welts on my body I looked ten pounds heavier.

At home I couldn't defend myself, but tonight I was about to kill some random muthafucka. What the hell was I thinking?

My gaze drifted to the circle of tall and undeniably dangerous-lookin' brothers and I felt the urge to be a part of a real family hit me again. If I showed these niggas I was down, then the sky was the limit.

The next thing I knew M. Dawg and I were shoved into the back of a black Cutlass, cruising the streets for my initiation victim. I had no idea at that time that not every member in the gang had to kill someone to get in. I found out much later that they had given me the task because they seriously thought that I would back down and run home with my tail tucked between my legs.

It was a full moon that night. I can't tell you how long we cruised around. Every time a potential vic was pointed out I would say, "He's not the one."

After a while, tempers flared in the car. The Disciples were more convinced than ever that I was just wasting their muthafuckin' time.

Hell, even my nigga M. Dawg was beginning to turn on me and frankly I wanted to go home, curl back under my bed.

Then I saw him.

He was strolling up Martin Luther King Boulevard in jeans, white T, and a jean jacket.

"All right!" One of the gang members clapped his hands, I think it was Zeke. "What about this muthafucka right here?"

The car slowed but my heart sped up while the gun grew heavier. I had ran out of excuses. The boy was alone, strolling like he had all the time in the world to get to wherever the hell he was going.

The heat in the car was incredible. Sweat had broken out across my forehead and was now dripping into my eyes. I even clung to the sudden thought that there was a good chance I would miss him. Shit. I ain't never shot a gun before. What were the chances?

Suddenly, a calm settled over me. There's no better way to describe it. I wasn't shakin' anymore and the gun felt as if it was merely an extension of myself. I lifted my extended arm out the window, aimed, and then pulled the trigger. Two quick shots; the gun's kickback didn't faze me.

The first bullet slammed into the kid's shoulder, spun him around to face the car. The second hit him dead in his chest, lifting him off the ground. The whole thing played out in slow motion. To this day I can't quite read the expression on Kadrian's face. Sometimes I think it was shock and others, a welcomed acceptance. When his body slammed onto the concrete, it felt as if the very earth cracked open and a few more demons from hell escaped their fiery prison.

"Aw shit! Aw shit!" someone shouted in raucous laughter. "This nigga did it."

Tires squealed and the car rocketed off into the night.

I bolt up in bed, my eyes wide and bugged-out while they try to adjust to the bedroom's dim lighting. I can't see shit and the only sounds I hear is my own labored breathing, my wild beating heart. It takes a few seconds but I soon make out the outline of the dressing room mirror and then finally the footboard.

Zoey's apartment.

I close my eyes and plop back down on the bed's pillows. Bentley Manor. I can't believe I'm back up in this shitty apartment complex, trapped and cornered by my past.

Zoey rolls toward me, sliding her hand up my chest and placing her head in the crook of my arm. She's been a bit clingy since I moved in. Of course, I've been wearing that pussy out, too. I've hit it in every room in this small-ass apartment and even tried out some freaky shit I've been dreamin' about since lockdown.

Zoey was down for it all, draining me so dry sometimes that I could hardly move.

Yeah, when things are good—it's good. But when we fight . . . shit gets crazy.

We both get crazy.

But I get dangerous.

I push the ugly fight we had ten years ago to the back of my mind and try to gently extract her from my arms.

It's too hot to cuddle.

I suck in a deep breath and hold off despair a little while longer. I toss the thin sheet off my body—this damn bedroom is hot as a damn oven. I need something to drink. I sit up once again and then roll up out of bed and grab my black boxers from off the floor. After I slide them on, I make my first pit stop in the hall bathroom. I pull up the toilet seat and take a long piss.

When I'm done, I flush and move over to the sink, wash my hands, lean forward, and throw some water on my face as well. Almost instantly I feel my body's temperature cool.

I reach for one of the folded towels from the back of the toilet. After I pat my face dry, I look up into the mirror and stare at a face that looks as if it's been chipped out of granite. I study my even brown skin and hard jawline and wonder if I look like my parents.

My eyes fall to the tattooed teardrops beneath my right eye. I'm going to need makeup to cover that up when I go out on job interviews. It's a good thing that the other tats across my body are easier to hide. The huge spiderweb on my shoulder is a popular prison tat letting brothers know I served hard time. The ones spread across my chest was a constant reminder of a life I wanted to forget.

A black Glock complete with a smoking tip was etched across my heart; underneath it the letters T.D. signified my gang affiliation. But the one in the center, the one that gave me the most heartache, spelled out as bold as you please the kind of man I used to be: KILLER.

Disgusted, I turn off the bathroom light and stroll to the kitchen. Unlike the other apartments up in Bentley Manor, Zoey keeps her shit tight and clean. By that I mean there are less rats and roaches. Still all the appliances are old and the pipes knocked whenever you turned on the water.

But shit, it's a place to stay.

After downing several glasses of water, I find myself in the living room on my knees praying to Allah for more strength and courage to face the demons still swirling in Bentley Manor.

The prayers don't come easy. Behind my closed eyelids I keep seeing dead faces—all of them by my hand.

No rest or peace for the wicked. It suddenly seems like my prayers are fallin' on deaf ears. It's enough to bring tears to my eyes.

"Demarcus?" Zoey's soft husky voice floats out to me a second before her hand lands on my shoulder. "Baby, how long have you been out here?"

Still on my knees I glance up at her, her appearance seeming almost angelic. I pull her close, lock my arms around her waist while I bury my face against her soft belly. The musky scent of our previous lovemaking drifts across my nose and I'm instantly hard.

"Let's go back to bed," she whispers.

I shake my head and rub my hands all over her thick booty. I don't want to go back to sleep. I don't want to go back and remember. I rather bury myself into the one good thing I have in my life.

My baby, Zoey.

"Stay out here with me," I say, pulling up her night-gown and trailing kisses across her belly and then the springy curls between her legs. I feel her tremble so I move my hands to slide between her thick thighs. They open up for me immediately and I slip my tongue in between her thick lips and savor her body's sweetness.

I moan. No one can convince me that she wasn't dipped in Godiva chocolate.

"Lay down on the floor."

She obeys without question. I hike her legs over my shoulder and I sink my tongue in as far as it will go and begin lapping her up.

Her sighs are like music to my ears.

She squirms and rotates her pussy against my face.

"You like that, baby?" I ask, sliding a finger into her ass and then going back to town on her hard center.

Her entire body quivers and I mop up every drop of juice when her first orgasm hits. Still, I keep going, lost in her taste.

"Please, baby. Please," she begs. "Fuck me! Fuck me now, Demarcus!"

She doesn't have to ask twice. I climb up her body and squeeze my thick shaft into her as gently as I can. I'm a nice nine inches but I'm thick as hell and in the past I had been known to send quite a few ladies to their doctor's office.

Zoey places her hand against my chest, silently urging me to hold up a few seconds while her body tries to adjust.

I try to be patient, but she feels so good right now. Her vaginal walls have clamped on to me like a velvet fist and my toes are curling and every breath she takes caresses my cock.

She grinds her hips and as I stroke her body to make squishing and sucking sounds.

Oh God. Oh God. This is heaven.

Oh yeah. I'm about to tear this shit up.

Small slices of moonlight slither through the venetian blinds and allow me to watch her bountiful breasts bounce and jiggle beneath me. My mouth dries out since we're now working up a black sweat and I lean forward and suck her fat titties.

Every part of her body tastes and feels so damn good. "DE-MAR-CUS, Oh!"

With her body clenching tighter and tighter, I forget to pull out and we cum at the same time; my body empties everything it has into her.

"I love you, baby." I mumble, pulling her close. I'm never going to fuck this shit up again.

Never.

9

The Playa

"Whaddup, Rhak."

I look out the open window of the car and give a head nod to some fool hollerin' at me. The cracked leather of the seat sticks to my legs and arms as I hop my ass out the car. This July heat makes me sweat like a damn slave. The air is busted and without Shaterica's ass to fix it, I'm ridin' hot as a motherfucker. Sometimes it feels like the motherfuckin' devil is sittin' on the dashboard laughin' at my ass.

As always the courtyard of Bentley Manor is packed. You never know just how many motherfuckers stay in a complex 'til it gets hot, especially after the sun went down and it cooled off a little bit. Two or three bodies are either leaning or sitting on just about every parked car. A shit-load of badass kids is either ballin' or playin' jump rope or some shit. Windows are open and some are lucky enough to be filled with box fans or small air conditioners.

I'm gettin' my box out of the trunk when I see them old bitches wavin' me over to them. I want to flip them nosy birds the bird, but I ain't stupid. I really ain't supposed to even be here with Shaterica in jail and me still living in her shit. I felt lucky as hell ain't nobody told the managers her ass been locked up for a month or they would evict her and then my ass would be on the street. Fuck the dumb shit. I gots to make me some damn money and these wannabe bitches 'round here gone eat up these fake-ass designer handbags I got in this box. For thirty bucks they could pretend they ass rockin' Gucci, Coach, and good ole Louis like them rich bitches.

With the box under my arm, I close the trunk and stroll over to them just as fine as I please in my new white T and Dickie shorts.

"How is Shaterica, Rhakmon?" The light one, Miz Osceola, asks as soon I stroll up to them. Her eyes all squinted the fuck up and looking at me like she ready to whup my ass.

I'm young but I ain't fuckin' dumb. I look all sad and shit. "I went to see her yesterday and she holdin' up pretty good. I'm workin' hard to get her a better lawyer than a public defender, you know?" Truth? I ain't been nowhere near that motherfucker since I dropped her the fuck off. On top of that when detectives came around Bentley Manor askin' people questions about Shaterica they questioned me too, but fuck that, I pretended like I ain't know shit about that bitch. Don't know her and don't want to know her. Oh, a playa like me ain't tryna get linked back to that shit.

Miz Cleo sucks her damn false-ass teeth. "Working? That would mean bein' up on somebody job and not ridin' around in that girl's car all day, ain't it?"

Miz Osceola nods her head as she leans forward in her chair to rest her fleshy arm on the tip of one of them damn bats they always got wit 'em.

See? Couple of nosy bitches.

Man, what the fuck ever. "I'll tell her y'all asked about her," I tell them before I turn away.

"You do that," one of them called behind me.

All them bullets flyin' around this motherfucker sometimes and ain't *one* manage to catch they ass while they sittin' there all the fuckin' time?

Shit, I got other shit on my mind . . . like money, money, and more money. I'm missing Shaterica's check like a motherfucker. I already took all the money she had out of her checking account—a debit card and a pin code is a damn good thing, especially since I had her purse.

As I head up the walkway and into the buildin', I see Delia up to her normal bullshit in the center of them young fuckers dealin' dope. I ain't got time for *that* shit. There's too many other ways to hustle and make money. Fuck always runnin' from the cops and crackheads naggin' you all day for a bump. Man, *shit* on that.

The door of the building slams behind me as I jog up the steps to the second floor. I ain't even got time to notice the faint scent of piss creepin' up from the corners. At the top of the stairs, I see a couple of hot-ass kids pressed up on each other in the corner. They so busy kissing and finger fuckin' that they ass don't even see me. The girl can't be no more than twelve with her legs spread open wide while the boy tryin' his hardest to grind all up against her.

I ain't hatin' so I keep on movin' past them. Shit, I done gots plenty of ass in stairwells, parked cars, school bathrooms, and everywhere else since I first started fuckin'. Young buck can't afford no hotel and if her hot ass willin' to give it up then he better go for what he knows.

I'm just about to unlock the door and stroll into the apartment when the door across the hall from me opens. I look over my shoulder and my eyes get big as shit. What . . . the . . . fuck?

"What's up wit you, Rhak?"

Polette, this fifty-year-old bitch lookin' like she headed toward seventy fast as hell, is standin' her whop-up ass in the doorway naked as fuck with a smile that shows her yellow-ass spacey teeth. Bitch mouth look like they filled up with open doors. And her body? I swallow hard to keep from throwin' up at the sight of her saggy-ass titties and long-ass coochie and underarms hair. I know some bitches that can cornrow her shit. Her stomach is flabby as fuck and she one of them bitches with those drumstick legs all big at top and skinny as shit at the bottom. Her eyes are yellow and watery from all the liquor she be fuckin' up and that played-out jheri curl is dry as fuck and gray as hell.

Is . . . this . . . bitch . . . crazy?

"Won't you come on in here and get some of dis here pussy?" she says, her voice slurring like crazy. I can't help but make a nasty-ass face when she kind of twirls her wide-ass hips. This the first time seein' a bitch naked makes my dick get smaller like it's tryna crawl up in me. For real.

"Bitch, please," I tell her before I walk into the apartment and slam the motherfuckin' door close behind me.

She been tryna holler at a nigga for a minute but she ain't never come at me like this before. What the fuck made her oogly ass think a fine motherfucker like me would give her ass the time of day? I wouldn't fuck that bitch with somebody else's dick. Fuck that. I gots to do a peephole check before I leave this damn apartment 'cause I ain't tryna to run up on *that* bullshit again.

I drop the box onto the peelin' fake-ass leather couch and I head for what I know is waitin' on me in the bedroom. The phone rings. Damn.

I snatch up the bright-ass pink cordless that feel and work just like the eight-dollar motherfucker that it is. "Whaddup?"

"You have a collect call from a correctional facility—"

Shaterica. I roll my eyes like a bitch as I punch the number one on the piece of shit phone so hard that the button stays pushed in. This bitch was taking a murder charge for me and the last thing I want is for her to tell the real, so damn right I take her calls. Especially since her sentencing was today and a nigga like me wanted to know just what the fuck all went on in court. It took a lot of sweet talk to convince her I should stay away for our plan to work. She 'bout a dumb ass.

"Hey, baby girl."

"Hey, Rhakmon. How you doin', baby?"

I flop down in the pleather armchair and feel the air from one of the cracks blow against the back of my damned leg. "Naw, fuck that, baby. It don't matter how I'm doin'. Whaddup wit you? What happened? You a'ight?"

The line gets real quiet for a long time.

Uh oh. "You there, baby girl?"

"I don't want to talk about it in here. Talk about something else. *Anything* fucking else."

The bedroom swings open with a whinin'-ass squeak. I look up to see my new bitch Shay walking her thick ass over to me in a pair of striped coochie cutter shorts and a sports bra that didn't do shit to hide her hard-ass nipples. I can tell from the look in her hazel eyes that she ready to fuck. Good, 'cause so am I.

"Uhm . . ." I try to think of some hood gossip to tell her but my mind goes blank as hell 'cause Shay stands between my open legs chewing on a piece of gum sexy as fuck as she looks down at me and works her shorts down over her hips. My dick gets hard at the sight of her fat-ass pussy with just a strip of hair runnin' down the middle.

She's my little secret. Just eighteen and ready to please

this nigga. I met her when I was hustlin' my bags down-town and for the last week her ass been right up in this apartment waitin' for me to come and give her all this good dick. Young and dumb—just the way I like them. Who knows where she told her momma she was stayin'. Who knows and who gives a fuck.

"Rhak? Rhak?"

"Yeah?" I shake my head tryna get right as I watch Shay turn around and jiggle her smooth caramel ass in a million different directions. I forget all about Shaterica's dumb ass.

Shay turns around again and massages her own tit-ties as she drops down to her knees and flips her fake-ass ponytail over her shoulder. She winks at me as she brought up them hands and works my hard-ass dick out of my baggy shorts. The feel of her hot hands on my dick makes my fuckin' heart jump in my chest and my ass get tight. Damn.

"Rhak!"

"Go ahead, I'm listening," I say into the phone, dis-tracted like a motherfucker cause Shay is licking me from my nuts to the tip of my thick dick. My legs shiverin' like crazy.

"I said they gave me ten years." Her voice is quiet and low. I barely hear her but I know she cryin'.

Shay's jaw is caved in from suckin' my dick so hard. If she keep up I'm a bust this nut right in her mouth. Fuck it. A nut is a nut.

"Hey, hold on one sec." I push the cordless down in between the cushions of the sofa, not even waitin' for her to answer.

"Toot that thing up, momma," I tell her, grabbin' her ponytail to pull her head back so that my dick is out her mouth.

She stands up and turns around again, reachin' behind herself to grab my dick tight as hell. My lips circle as she lowers her pussy down onto it. Tattooed across her lower back are the words:

"Whose is it?"

Well, I don't know whose it was last week but until *I* get tired of her ass, the pussy is *mine*. I bite my bottom lip and lift my hips up to push my dick up deeper inside of her 'til it feel like I'm tappin' on the bottom of that pussy.

"Uhmmm," she moans in the back of her throat before she grabs her knees and starts riding this dick backward. Her grind is slow and easy. Her pussy is tight and wet.

Damn!

I bring my hands up to squeeze her titties and I ain't gone lie, this bitch had sweat poppin' off my damn forehead and my heart was beatin' so hard it felt like a motherfucker was squeezin' my heart in his fuckin' hand. Every time this chick worked her hips around her pussy would clamp down on my dick and then ease up and down on it like she milkin' my shit.

I reach between her thick-ass legs with one hand and tease her wet clit. The deeper I put pressure on the motherfucker the more her body jerks, lettin' this nigga know I'm on the right spot. The pussy gets wetter and hotter. So fuckin' hot. I can feel every ridge of that pussy like a damn clamp.

Shee-it. I might be in fuckin' love with this bitch.

Still on my dick she shoves my hands away and turns around to face me. She pushes me back against the couch and leans forward until her pussy lips are on the tip of my dick. Still chewin' her gum like she got all day, she smiles and leans her head down to lick my mouth as she pops her hips. Her pussy is workin' the tip of my dick.

I ain't gone lie. That shit feels good as a motherfucker. She gone make me cum, and I know from the hot feel of her walls clutchin' down on my dick that she gone cum, too. Good. The *best* nut in the world is when a nigga and his bitch cum together.

She guides one of her titties to my mouth and I circle my tongue around it. Her body shakes and shit and I know it feel good to her. So I do it again. And again. And again. Until she ridin' me so hard that I'm scared this bitch gone stroke the fuck out.

I suck her tittie so hard that the whole motherfucker is in my mouth. It's salty from our sweat but it tasted good as hell to me as my dick explodes a load of cum up inside her. Shee-it. My balls get tight as fuck and my thighs shakin' like a bitch as I cum so hard that my guts hurt.

She gets up and drops to her knees to suck my hard dick like she love the taste of my nut. My mouth opens and shit and I'm scared this bitch gone kill my ass as she works her lips and jaws like she hungry for my shit. And she keep goin' until I ain't got shit left to come out this motherfucker.

I don't know who taught this bitch to fuck but I thank him like a motherfucker.

She sits back and smiles up at me, still chewin' on that piece of gum. I feel like kissin' this bitch since the fuck was so good, but not with all my cum drippin' from her mouth and chin. "Yo, go wash up and let me finish this call," I tell her. I ain't barely got the energy to move and right now a nigga really just want to sleep.

She don't say shit and hops right to her feet, grabs her shorts, and trots right into the bathroom like I told her.

I try to get my breathin' and shit together as I dig down into the chair for the phone. I ain't worryin' about Shaterica overhearin'. You can barely hear shit on that cheap motherfucker when it's to your ear.

"I'm back, baby," I tell her ass as I fling my limp dick back inside my boxer shorts. The scent of Shay's pussy is still in the air. *Humph.* I wish I could swallow that motherfucker.

"What you doin'?" Shaterica asks.

"Somebody was at the door."

"Oh."

The line went quiet for a minute before she speaks again. I'm fallin' back and lettin' her take the lead. I know that ten years is still on her mind.

"You know they tried to get me to admit I was lying about shooting him," she says.

I frown. "But you stuck to the story?"

"Yeah, I told them he tried to carjack me. That's why I got a manslaughter charge and not murder."

"You did good, baby." My voice is smooth as melted chocolate up in this piece. "You did real good for *us*."

10

The Pimp

This father-knows-best shit is for the birds. Can't a pimp get some peace in his own house? Ever since Corrine moved into my crib, it's been like World War III up in that mutherfucka. It's been little less than a month and Renee is still giving me the evil eye every time I roll up in the house, poppin' off at the mouth whenever Corrine is in sight and downright being disrespectful 24/7. Hell, Destiny has been actin' more like a stepmom than Renee's selfish ass.

I'm doing all I can not to bitch-slap her back into line because I know most of this shit is about her being hurt.

But goddamn. Let the shit go. The girl is here now and there's not a damn thing I can do about it. So while she's throwin' a fit, tryna teach me a lesson by spendin' up my cash, I decide to hang out at one of my lucrative adventures: Club Diamond.

Before you get it twisted, Club Diamond is not your regular run-of-the-mill strip joint. Everything I do, I do with class, and my club is the classiest spot up in the A-T-L.

I have the juiciest Georgia peaches ridin' my poles and gettin' niggas wet and makin' it rain all day, every day. And if you're one of the lucky mutherfuckas to get up in my VIP section, the rules are: *There are no rules.* Anything goes, baby. Your every fantasy is fulfilled.

Everyone who is anyone rolls up in here. From the latest rap stars to high profile politicians (using the back door, of course). My girls pop pussies and empty niggas' wallets. Believe that.

Usually, I float through Diamonds once maybe twice a week, but with all the domestic drama I'm going through I've been here nearly every day just to get a little peace.

Tonight is no different. The crowd is definitely jumpin' and filled to the max.

Just how I like it.

I'm sitting in my reserve seat in the VIP, casing the area and smiling at niggas that are getting private lap dances or gettin' their dicks wet while stuffing hundred-dollar bills any and everywhere. I'm actually feeling pretty good.

"Mind if I join you?"

I glance to my right and I'm more than surprised to see Renee beaming down at me. I ain't in the mood for her mouth.

"Please?" she adds. "I promise I'll be good."

I nod for her to take a seat.

She smiles and sits down. At thirty-seven, Renee still has a body as tight and as right as any Hollywood bitch walking the red carpet. The classy short number she selected to wear tonight gives me an immediate hard-on.

Within seconds of her sitting down, a waitress appears and places her favorite martini in front of her.

"What brings you out?" I ask, keepin' my voice reserved.

"I came to apologize," she says sweetly—a little too sweetly, if you want to know the truth. She's up to something, but for peace, I'm willing to take a bite of whatever the hell she's offering.

"I know I've been giving you hell this past month," she says. "About your *daughter*," she spat, as if it left some kind of foul taste in her mouth. "You know, I was thinking. We don't *really* know whether she's yours."

I roll my eyes. "She's mine, Renee. She has my eyes. And you know I used to hook up with Tracy on the regular." It doesn't bother me to throw up my infidelities to my wife. She knows how I get down just as I know how she gets down.

"Well, can't we find her momma and give her back? We can hire a private dick or something." She sulks.

"I thought you said that you were going to be nice?"

"I am being nice," she says stonily. "I'm not screaming, am I?"

That much is true. "Look, Renee. She's my daughter.

She doesn't have anywhere else to stay. I'm not going to just throw her out on the street. You can get that shit out-cha head." I draw a deep breath. This is exactly why my ass ain't home right now. I'm tired of having this same damn argument with her.

"I don't want her in my house," she stresses through gritted teeth.

My eyebrows spring up at that shit. "Whose house? You better step back in line." I lean over the table. "You know I don't take orders from no mutherfucka—and that includes you. So check your tone and remember who the fuck you're talking to," I hiss. I've put up with enough of this bullshit. "She's *my* daughter and I say she fuckin' stays at my mutherfuckin' crib as long as she wants. Are we clear?"

Renee's expression changes from surprise to outrage. I've treated her like the queen bee for so long that she's forgotten I can knock her off that throne at any mutherfuckin' time.

"You're actually gonna choose that li'l bitch over me?"

I don't even remember *thinkin'* about slappin' her; I just react and feel the sting of her face meeting my hand. When her head snaps back, I allow a wave of satisfaction to wash over me.

"You got something else smart to say—or do you want everyone in this club to watch me beat your ass?" I ask. "Corrine is my daughter and she fuckin' stays. End. Of. Story."

Recovering, she glares at me and touches her now bleeding lip. After a few dabs of her cocktail napkin, she's good as new.

"You two look like you may need a referee," Destiny says, arriving at our table. She's wearing a shimmering silver dress. As always there's very little evidence to suggest that she is a he.

More fire leaps into Renee's eyes.

I tell Destiny to have a seat before Renee tells her to go away.

Look. I'm not an idiot. I know my wife doesn't exactly care for my relationship with Destiny. Sometimes I wonder if her anger isn't more rooted to the fact that she herself is still attracted to Destiny aka Destin—my best friend who'd paid me his allowance to fuck her behind the school's bleachers.

She probably thinks I've forgotten, but I remember how Destin used to tear that ass up and have her speakin' in tongues.

"Don't tell me that Little Miss Sunshine still have you two stressed out."

"I wish you would stop calling her that," I say, rollin' my eyes and reaching for my own drink.

"What?" She shrugs. "I think it sort of suits her—at least the fake persona she running on you. I don't buy that good-girl act she's peddling. I think she has more of your personality than you realize."

"Please. You don't know anything about her."

"Neither do you," Destiny charges back. "The girl has been up in your house for the last month and you've barely said more than hi and bye to her. If you're going to ignore the girl, you might as well just send her back to her momma."

Renee's eyes light up as she sets her drink down. "Well, I'll be damned. Destin and I actually agree on something for a change."

"Both of you can suck my dick." I'm tired of this shit.

"I'll be more than happy to. You wanna do it here or upstairs in your office?" Destiny asks.

I know she meant it as a joke, but my dick gets hard again at the very thought of a ménage à trois right about now. I indulge every now and then but the three of us haven't gotten down together in a while.

"Ooh. What's that sparkle in your eye?" Destiny asks, sliding her hand into my crotch. "Don't tell me my favorite fantasy man has a fantasy of his own he's not fulfilling."

One side of my lips curls upward.

"Well, I'm game if you are," Destiny says, perking up and then glancing over at Renee. "What about you?"

Renee hesitates.

"Or maybe you rather I have him all to myself tonight," Destiny baits. "You know a fierce bitch like me can rock his world all by my damn self."

Renee's chin tilts upward. "Anything you can do, I can do better."

When it came to me, they often turned very territorial. Fuck it. I love the attention.

"But I was in the middle of a private conversation with my husband," Renee hisses.

I suck air between my teeth and roll my eyes. "That discussion is closed, Renee," I tell her.

She gives me a look like she wants to challenge me again but instead reaches for her drink and takes a long sip. "I never ask you for much," she mumbles.

I don't actually hear the words over the music but I read her lips. What she says is true. Throughout the years, Renee has always done everything I've ever asked her to do and there's not a single day I don't wonder why. The only thing I can come up with is: when women love, they love hard.

But I'm no good and she knows it.

If Renee wants to quit this life and leave, she can, I won't stop her. I'll give her a kiss on the lips and a smack on the ass and wish her luck.

Maybe she knows that, too. So instead, she chooses to stay by my side through thick and thin or rather through stacked cash and a long line of hos. All she asks is to remain my number one girl.

And she is.

And will always be.

"Anytime you want to get off this ride, you can," I tell her.

Her eyes shoot up. "Is that what you really want?" she tosses back at me.

Hell, naw! This conversation has grown more serious than I'm comfortable with because in the midst of all this craziness, Renee has always been the rock that centers me. Renee is and will forever be Home.

"I want you to do you, boo," I say, playing this shit off but hoping she reads in my eyes that I want her to stay and play her position.

Slowly, she nods her head.

Destiny wiggles impatiently beside me. "So are we going to do this shit or what? I'm all dressed up with nobody to fuck."

I lift a curious brow at my wife, letting her know that I'm down.

Renee's gaze shifts between the two of us. I know she's battling her possessive nature. She's not jealous of any of the other girls that float in and out of my bed, but Destiny is different and she knows it.

"Fine," she agrees and then drains the rest of her drink. "Let's go."

My private office slash bedroom above the club has an excellent view of everything that's going on from the bottom floor to the VIP section. It's surrounded by glass but tinted so I can look out but no one can see inside.

My space is furnished with top-of-the-line shit and even has a large round rotating bed for emergency fuck sessions and auditions, carpet that doubles as a mattress, mirrors strategically placed, funky lighting, and even the best AK-47 bud that can get you high after one toke.

I follow the sway of my two best girls' hips while two of my best bodyguards take post outside my door. I hit one button and the club's music disappears; I hit another one and the best fuck music from Teddy Pendergrass flows from my private sound system.

Renee is the first one to roll up into my arms and lay a fat wet one on me. I'm already in paradise sucking my number one girl's fat lips and rubbing up on her firm diamond-studded breasts when Destiny wraps her strong and powerful mouth around my cock.

Now why can't I have this peace and harmony 24/7? This is how a pimp should always get down. In no time I peel Renee out of her clothes and plop one of her breasts back into my mouth.

I'm sucking and biting while rocking my hips against Destiny's mouth. Whenever she hits a particular sweet spot, I growl out *oh shit!* against Renee's breasts. When it really gets good, I place my hand against the back of Destiny's perfectly weaved head and grind my shit to the back of her tight-assed throat. Destiny is like a super power vacuum and sucks my nut up from the tips of my toes.

In the spirit of competition, Renee pulls her succulent breast from my mouth and lowers onto her knees so she can get a taste of her baby as well. I plop down in the chair behind me and then watch my girls lick and stroke my dick like it's the last candy cane on Christmas day. Each mouth feels different and off da chain.

"My best girls," I whisper, and lovin' how my cock looks like a glazed chocolate éclair.

My nut sac tingles and Renee finally gives up the ghost and starts polishing my balls. Shit. I need them to start doin' this shit on the regular. Destiny hits my sweet spot just as Renee's warm tongue drifts to the crack of my ass. The results: my gooey hot cum shoots out of my cock like Fourth of July fireworks. It splashes against Destiny's face like an abstract painting and then drips down into Renee's hair. But that doesn't stop them from lapping my shit up and begging me for more.

My ten inches remain rock hard and ready to go. On the side table, Renee pulls out a condom and slips that mutherfucka on me so she could be the first to ride. I know I've fucked this pussy a million times, but there's something about the way Renee works her shit that gets me excited each and every time.

And she knows it.

The minute she stands, I see my diamond trademark above the slit of her pussy. That's my shit. It will always be my shit. I smile and she knows exactly what I'm thinking.

"Who's your number one girl?"

"You are, baby."

Renee eases down on me and I close my eyes relishing the feel of home. I know this pussy like I know the back of my hand. Her inner walls are like the finest silk and her body's so hot my toes curl in ecstasy. In no time, she's working that pussy like a pro and I'm concentrating like a mutherfucka to prolong this nut.

It ain't easy, especially when I feel Destiny's mouth and tongue lapping at my and Renee's sex juices while positioned in between us.

After a while I gain control of my breathing and manage to open my eyes to enjoy the sights and sounds before me.

Destiny moves back and starts to get undressed. When she finally frees her own thick eight-inch cock, Renee reaches out and strokes it while maintaining her bounce on my dick.

Destiny just smiles. "You want some of this shit, don't you, bitch?"

Renee doesn't answer, she just continues to pump Destiny's cock and lick her lips.

Destiny pulls back, grabs a condom and a stool and climbs up and then offers up her hard dick. Renee takes to it like a babe to a tit. Destiny throws her head back and pure bliss covers her face. Seeing Renee stuffed this way brings my second nut to a head.

"Goddamn, bitches," I groan and then shoot my shit off. But this party is just getting started.

After a condom change, we tumble over to the bed where I get a good meal out of Renee's pussy while Destiny continues to feed her his cock. It isn't long before Renee's squirting all over the place.

Needing some more pussy, I climb up and order Destiny to fuck Renee from behind. We rock the shit out of her hard body while her inner cream coats our dicks.

"Aw, shit," Renee screams; her pussy starts smacking back.

"Fuck. Goddamn. Mutherfucker!" I yell as my nut gushes out of me and supersoaks my condom and drips out of her body. Hours later, we drift off to sleep.

Peace at last. Peace at last. Thank God Almighty a pimp has peace at last.

11

The Dealer

"Call me sometime. My name is Jessica."

I look down at the ripped piece of register tape being pushed in my hand. My eyes lift up to the sweet, deep-brown face looking up at me. Looks like this salesgirl is looking for more from me than a boost in her Nordstrom's commission. I smile at her as she gives my palm a little scratch before she walks away with a lick of her lips. That scratch let me know that she has an itch that she wants me to scratch.

My eyes stay locked on that ass as she walks back over to Quilla, who is shopping it up . . . on my ass of course. Fuck it. My eyes stay locked on the salesgirl's apple-bottom ass in the black dress pants she's wearing. But even as I enjoy the view I ball the number up and toss it into the wastepaper basket by the register.

The last thing I need is another female in my life. Between Quilla, the twins, and a few random chicks, my dick couldn't take no more. Fuck that. There is such a thing as too much pussy. I got into the game to get girls but now I got *too* many bitches.

I glance at my camel-leather Gucci watch before I slip my hands into the pockets of my loose-fitting linen shorts. My ass is ready to be out. I only like shopping when I'm taking care of my own needs. Standing around just waiting to pay while somebody else spends my money ain't a bit of fucking fun.

Plus, I'm waiting on a call from Usher signaling me that he picked up the latest shipment of weight from our contact. With nearly a hundred grand in hard dope on his back, I didn't trust none of our usual runners, so Usher volunteered to do it himself.

I walk over to one of the mirrors on the wall and smooth a wrinkle out of the bright white Hilfiger T I wore over a wifebeater. I cup the bill of the linen cap and pull it down lower over my eyes. My jewelry is gleaming from my neck and wrist. My grille is shiny. My set is tight. A lot of bitches tell me I look like Nelly. I don't really see it but fuck it. Whatever helps make the pussy wetter.

"Uhm, excuse me, your wife wants you."

I frown as I turn around. There's the sexy salesgirl still looking like she ready to fuck me on the spot. She slick as hell as she pulls her print blouse down slightly to flash me the tops of her cleavage. One full breast is tattooed *Lick* and the other one says *Suck*.

I'm not even letting her bullshit blow up my head because bitches these days see a nigga like me with cash flow and that's what make them so hot. It took my young ass a minute to get it but now I'm straight. She wants to be Quilla and have her nigga take her on a shopping spree because knowing Quilla she let it be known that I'm paying.

"She's not my wife," I tell her as I follow her over to the line of dressing rooms.

The salesgirl shrug like she didn't care either way. The look she gives me lets me know she don't give a fuck about Quilla and me and what kind of relationship we have. She want me for herself.

I walk into the dressing room area and see Quilla peeking her head out from behind a wooden door in the back. She smiles at me, happy as hell.

"So you my wife?" I ask her as I walk into the room with her. There are clothes everywhere and knowing Quilla she wants it all. Knowing me, she'll get it.

Quilla is a damn good girlfriend. My Queen. My First Lady. She's about as close to getting married as I will get for a while. She puts up with my shit. She listens to me when I just want to talk. She fucks me like she my personal whore but reps me to the fullest in the streets. She's smart as hell and works for the county as a court clerk. She can cook. Fuck me. Cherish me. King me. Love me the best she can. I know that sound all corny and shit but in this game, it's hard to find someone to love you for you.

I learned that the hard way with my last girl, but that's the past. I'm not fucking with *that* shit.

I know I'm wrong for how much I fuck around on Quilla. She's a good girl and she don't deserve it, but money brings on mad bitches and sometimes it's hard as hell to ignore a big ass and a smile.

I turn around just as the dressing room door clicks as she closes it. Quilla is dressed in nothing but a "fuck me" see-through teddy and her gold Gucci heels. She is looking cocky as hell as she slowly turns in front of me— knowing that she looks good from head to toe and front to back. "How much of my money you spending today?" I ask her, feeling just as fucking cocky as she do.

She shakes her shoulder length curly weave and licks her glossy lips as she walks up to me. "I don't know," she says carelessly with a shrug before she wraps her arms around my neck and runs her teeth over my bottom grill with a purr. "I *do* know that the little bitch out there better not get herself hurt."

Uh-oh. "What you talkin' 'bout, Quilla?"

She slides her tongue inside my mouth just as she slides her hand down to massage my dick until it's hard in her hand. "Don't worry 'bout it, Boo," she whispers into my mouth before she circles my tongue with hers. "It ain't your fault she scandalous."

Quilla don't miss shit. I'm still surprised she ain't caught up with most of my shit. "You picked out everything you want?" I ask, changing the subject.

"Yup," she says calm as hell as she pulls on her Donna Karan safari dress. Too calm.

I open the door while she slides on her black Gucci stunner shades and puts her gold tote on her shoulder. She looks the role of my queen. The head bitch in charge. I ain't gone lie. I like that about her.

As soon as we step out the dressing room area, the salesgirl brings her ass over to us. Shee-it. I'm nervous as hell that Quilla about to straight-slap this chick.

"Jessica, could you get everything out that last dressing room. We'll take it all." Quilla gives her a smile that is nothing but sweetness.

Say what?

Jessica the salesgirl's eyes get big as shit and I know Quilla just hit my pockets hard. Just a few minutes later, Jessica rolls an entire rack filled with clothes out of the dressing room toward the register.

My Nextel rings and I flip it open. Usher. "Whaddup." I see Quilla's eyes cut over to me as I turn and walk away from her. "Done?"

"Done," Usher answers.

Enough said. As soon as I drop Quilla home, I'm headed straight to the spot to finish handling business.

I walk back over to Quilla and I know she dying to ask me who was on the phone, but she don't, thank God. Ain't shit worse than a naggin'-ass, nosy-ass woman. I've told her ass that plenty of times. Maybe she finally fucking getting it.

"Now, Jessica, I need to speak with your manager."

Jessica's baby browns look at Quilla and then me and then back to Quilla again. "Is there a problem?" she asks, all nervous and shit.

Quilla bends down and reaches into the wastepaper basket. She rises back up and flings the scrap of paper with Jessica's name and number on it into her face. "If you think your little slick ass gone make a commission off this here sale, you crazy. Now go get your manager to ring . . . me . . . up and then I advise you to give me fifty feet."

I just drop my head and wipe my hand over my mouth to keep from smiling. *Humph.* Quilla don't miss shit.

Bentley Manor is important as hell to my business. All of these little foot soldiers out here work for me but they had to go through so many motherfuckers before they even got back to me that I know some of them don't even know who really runs the show. Shit, most people don't even know where I stay. I like it that way. Last thing I need is for one of these fools to get locked up and sign indictments against me.

So far. So good. But Maleek thought he was above the law and now he doing ten, fed time. How long would my luck or my ability to stay ahead of the game last?

I pull my black-on-black Tahoe through the open gates of Bentley Manor. I don't bother to get out. I fuck with a couple tricks out here who don't want nothing but a new pair of Uptowns or a whack-ass, fifty-dollar hairdo. I ain't in the mood tonight. I got other shit on my mind.

"You think she came up in here, Ush?" I look over at him sitting in the passenger seat, his eyes locked on the people hanging outside the complex through my black tint.

He nods. His face is all serious because he know how serious the shit he told me is.

By the time I made it to the spot, Usher had made sure the dope was cut, bagged up, and distributed. He didn't waste any time pulling me outside to tell me that my ex, Candy, was on the block strung the fuck out and begging them hot boys for a free hit. That shit damn near knocked me off my feet.

Candy and me went out for three years and I can't front that I loved her . . . up until the day I walked in on her fucking some Mexican dude in my bed. I looked past her ass being a stripper before we met. I looked past her shady rep on the street. I looked past the way she used to run through my money. I looked past her clubbing damn near Thursday through fucking Sunday. I even looked past the way she could smoke a half ounce of weed by her damn self, but I couldn't look past that.

I tossed her ass the fuck out of my apartment and last I heard she moved to North Carolina with Paco, Taco, or what the fuck ever his name was.

Have I thought about her in the last year? Hell, yeah.

Have I wondered where her crazy ass was? Most def.

But did I ever imagine her strung out on drugs? Never.

I can't front that its been fucking with me ever since Usher told me about it. Really, I shouldn't give a damn about her, but I do. I shouldn't want to see her, but I do.

"I made sure the word was out to call me if they see her and not to sell her shit."

I nod at Usher's words even as I reverse the Tahoe out of a parking spot. I use my free hand to turn up the radio and soon Shawty Lo's "Dunn Dunn" fills every inch of the space. With all the kids running around here I had to be careful I didn't run one the fuck over. I catch sight of the building Maleek and Aisha used to live in—the same building where one of her johns sliced her the fuck up because the pussy drove him crazy.

I shake my head to get thoughts of her out of my mind. I got enough female drama popping off right now. Worrying about what Aisha is doing with herself is big-time unnecessary right now.

As I roll out of Bentley Manor on my twenty-two-inch blacked-out rims, Usher lit a Newport. "Candy looked real bad, man. I mean bad. Like damn, what the fuck, you know?"

"So all that flyness she was about . . . just *gone*?" As I pull the truck to a stop at the red light I look over at my friend.

Usher locks his eyes with mine. "Gone," he stresses.

I shift my eyes to the Circle K gas station on the right. I frown when I see a tall skinny female holding a baby in one arm and swinging her other one like crazy in the face of one of my foot soldiers. Candy is tall. Tall enough to look my six-foot-one skinny ass dead in the eye whether we was fucking or fighting.

"That's her, Kaseem," Usher says, reaching over to slap my arm with the back of his hand twice.

"I already see her," I tell him, shifting the Tahoe into the right lane and turning into the Circle K parking lot.

As soon as Usher steps out of the Tahoe behind me he lights a fat blunt. I make a note to remind him later that not only didn't I want nobody smoking that shit in my ride, I didn't want nobody carrying that shit in my ride. It's that kind of dumb shit—traffic stops, personal stash of weed, roadblocks—that gets a big-time nigga like me caught all the time for bigger shit. Major shit.

As I walk up to her I can smell the funk on her a foot away. Her reddish-orange weave is matted and her tracks are hangin' loose. Her clothes are dingy and there's a nasty-ass blood spot on the seat of her jeans. The baby in her arms got more fat than she do. This head beggin' my boys for a hit is the woman I loved like crazy for three fucking years. What the fuck happened?

"Whaddup, Candy?" I call over to her as I stand behind her.

She turns and the darkness around her eyes still don't match the spots all over her face. Where there ain't no spots, her once brown skin is grayish and ashy. Her lips are white and cracked. She looks like the walking dead.

"Whassup, Kaseem," she says, shifting her eyes away from me as she puts her baby on her thin shoulder. "It's good to see you."

I can tell she is embarrassed and that makes me feel a little better. It makes me feel like all hope ain't lost for her because at least she still got shame. It's when they lose shame that there ain't no hope for these heads.

"I wish I could say it's good to see you, Candy." I can't be nothing but up front.

The fellas leaning against the side of the Circle K suddenly start walking away from us. I know without question that Usher signaled for them to bounce. I look over my shoulder and see him leading them inside the store.

She looks at me like she wants to spit in my face. "Don't judge me, Kaseem."

"Don't embarrass me, Candy," I shot right back at her ass.

"Embarrass?" She makes this funny noise in the back of her throat as she shifts the baby in her arms.

I look at the baby and back up at her. "That your baby?"

Now she looks at me like I'm stupid as hell. "No, motherfucker, I'm babysitting."

She still got that smart-ass mouth. "You think a mother should be out hustling for dope with her baby?" I couldn't help but sound fucking disgusted.

The baby starts crying as she steps up to me. "Who the fuck is you to test my fucking motherhood!" she shouts in my face. The smell of her breath—that rotten cabbage and dog shit mix—makes me sick to my stomach and lets me know the bitch ain't brushed her teeth in a hot minute.

"A slow motherfucker can see that the last thing your ass need is a child," I shot back in between holding my breath to keeping from swallowing down hers.

The baby's cries get louder and louder and I don't miss the little crowd circling us. I don't like a scene but Candy's ass looking like the fucking Crypt Keeper is freaking me out.

"So you perfect now, Kaseem? You look at me and you can't handle it but you pushin' that shit, though. Makin' all that loot so you can ride in your Tahoe and your Cadillac and your Mustang. Oh, I heard about you Mr. Big-Timer. All your diamond jewelry. Your designer clothes. Your big-time bitches at your side. All of these little wannabes lookin' up to your ass . . . all because you slingin' the shit I smoke. Don't look down your your nose at me, motherfucker. You makin' mad money off people like me."

I ain't gone lie. Her words hit home, but I refuse to give her the upper hand.

"Candace, where you staying at? Let me give some money for your baby—"

She laughs and something about it sounds crazy. "*My* baby?" she asks, walking back and forth in front of me as she laughs like she got some secret. "*My* baby."

For a second I imagine this crazy bitch throwing the baby to the ground like she spiking a football or throwing it out in the middle of traffic. I heard about dumb shit like that in the news but I wasn't even trying to be a witness to that bullshit. I reach out and snatch the baby from her arms.

She whirls at me and just laughs until she is bent over with her hands on her knees. "My baby. No, mother-fucker, try *our* baby."

I look down at the baby in my arms. I can't deny that he has my eyes. My son? I look up at her and see the moment this bitch gets an idea. That shit like in the cartoons when the bulb goes off. Still, I'm surprised as hell by her words.

"Give me ten grand and he's yours."

Now I *know* this bitch is crazy.

12

The Killer

"I'm sorry, but that position has been filled."

I drop my head in my hands and expel a long breath. It's the same shit, different day. I've been out the joint for damn near a month and have yet to find a good job . . . hell, any job. I'm not qualified to do much, even with the GED I obtained in the clink.

I know it's not my interviewing skills. Each time I go in, with my tats covered, I have the people eating outta my hand. It's when they get to *the box* when shit changes—the box where you check whether you've ever been convicted of a felony.

Mutherfuckas always change up then.

The interviews come to a screeching halt and I'm shown the door with the promise of *We'll call you*—which they never do.

"Look, Mr. Stewart. I'm just looking for a chance," I say, just shy of begging. "I know I can do the work."

"Like I said, the position has been filled, Mr. Jones."

Exhaling another breath, I nod against the phone. "A'ight. Thank you for your time." I hang up and crash back against the couch. As I look around the small, tidy apartment, I can't stop feeling like a worthless piece of shit. How in the hell can I call myself a man when Zoey is the only one with a decent job?

Every morning, Monday through Friday, she climbs out of bed and goes to work at a private doctor's office as a medical assistant somewhere in Midtown. She's only been working there for the past seven months. She had taken some courses at a school that had guaranteed job placement when she graduated.

Lately, all she's been talking about is saving up to buy a house within the next year. We can move out even faster if I land a job, too.

IF.

I know my being here is putting a strain on her finances. A big brother like me is puttin' a hurtin' on the grocery bill alone.

I'm tryin'. But the shit ain't workin'.

I hit the pavement and the bus system every day. There's gotta be someone out there willing to take a chance on an ex-con.

One thing, I make sure that the crib remains nice and clean for my baby. Dishes done. Floors vacuumed. Beds made. I gotta contribute some kind of way.

After a few deep breaths I shake my head clean of negative thoughts and reach for the newspaper spread out on the coffee table and scan the want ads again.

My first week out I applied for office entry jobs. The second week, I downgraded to service jobs. Now I call for any and every thing. Hell, illegal mutherfuckas stand a better chance than my ass getting hired.

The phone rings and I glance over.

UNKNOWN NUMBER.

I move away, rolling my eyes. Another bill collector, begging for money we don't have. Zoey explained that she'd run into a few credit card problems a few years back. Bankruptcy and credit counselors cost money, so Zoey handled it the ghetto way: wait seven years until that shit rolls off your credit. Being Zoey's man, I wish I could help solve her financial problems, but I ain't got a pot to piss in let alone have five to put on a bill.

Frustrated, I stand and head toward the kitchen for a much needed beer. The answer machine picks up the call and a strong feminine voice booms into the apartment.

"Yes. This message is for Demarcus Jones. This is Marsha Harding, your new parole officer."

"Oh shit!" I stop in my tracks.

"Mr. Jones, you had an appointment with me this morning and you failed to show up."

Fuck! Was that shit today?

"As you know, Mr. Jones, failure to appear for your appointments can result in your parole being revoked and a bench warrant issued for your arrest."

I rush over to the door and grab my jacket just as the phone call disconnects. However, I halt in my tracks when I nearly collide into Tonya Gainey, an old trick and unfortunately the baby momma to my twelve-year-old son.

"I should have known your sorry ass would be here," she blast up at me. She's all of five foot three with the same tight curves from way back.

"I can't talk to you right now, Tonya. I gotta make a run."

Tonya totally ignores me and Bogarts her way into the apartment. "Where yo girl at?" she asks at the top of her voice, looking around.

"Tonya, we're gonna have to do this another time. I really got to make a run."

"I don't give a fuck about what *you* gotta do," she says, looking me up and down like she's daring me to jump bad.

My anger flares at her determined disrespect. "Zoey is not here right now," I tell her after counting to ten inside my head. "She's at work."

"Ha!" Her head rocks back. "Let me guess. Your sorry ass is just up here, leeching off her while she busts her ass."

"Tonya," I say, my patience nearing its end. "What do you want?"

"What the fuck do you think I want?" Her hands straddle her hips. "I want my mutherfuckin' money, otherwise known as back child support. At least while your ass was locked up I was gettin' your sorry-ass work furlough checks. Since they've let yo black ass out, I ain't been getting shit—and yo kid cost money. Not that you've even tried to see his ass since you've been out."

"I tried to call—"

"Don't give me that bullshit. You just want to forget about me and Marctavious. You're too busy lying up here like a nigga with a slave."

Here we go. I knew we were gonna have this conversation sooner or later. At the moment, I wish it could be later. "Tonya, I'm trying to get you your money. You're gonna have to give me a little more time."

"I ain't gotta do shit but stay black and die, mutherfucker. *You,* on the other hand, have to get me my money or they'll take your ass back to jail. Marctavious is twelve years old and school starts next month. I didn't come here to hear about your problems. I came for my fuckin' money."

"I don't have any money to give you," I try to reason with her. "I'm looking for a job."

"What—standing around up here all damn day?" She looks around the apartment again. "What—you think Mr. Opportunity is just going to knock on the door?"

"I've been looking for a job since I've been out." I grind my teeth, struggling to talk to her like a civilized adult. "It hasn't been easy."

Tonya's high cackle stops me short. "You think it's been easy for me trying to take care of your kid for the past ten years by myself? Where the fuck were you when I was dealing with ear infections, running noses, shitty diapers, day care, groceries, school clothes. The list is endless. You didn't give a fuck about me when you were slinging and hustling with that pathetic two-bit gang you used to run around with. Maybe you should ask them for my mutherfuckin' money."

"Tonya—"

"And let's not forget your main ho Zoey that you conveniently forgot to tell me about when you were lying up in my bed."

"Tonya, I'm going to get you your money." I hear footsteps coming up the building's hallway but it doesn't register with me until Zoey is standing in the doorway.

Tonya instantly straightens up, her hood attitude chilled out for a moment.

I look at Zoey. "Hey, baby," I say.

"What in the hell is she doing here?"

"We were just talking," I say, not liking the suspicion creeping into her face.

Tonya's gaze rakes over Zoey in her medical scrubs. "Look like she has a good damn job. Maybe you should ask her for my damn money."

Zoey's hands settles onto her hips. "Excuse you?"

Tonya just ignores her. "Demarcus, get me my money." She heads for the door, glances Zoey up and down, and waits for her to move so she can leave the apartment.

Zoey shifts so that she blocks the entire doorway. "I know your momma taught you some manners."

"Excuse you," Tonya says.

It's the wrong answer, but at this point I can tell my baby just wants her ass gone. Zoey steps aside, but we both catch Tonya's departing words: "Fat bitch."

In a blink, Zoey was on her ass like white on rice. "I gotcha fat bitch." She grabs Tonya's ponytail and rips the mutherfucker clean off and then lands a couple of blows upside her head.

"How the fuck you gonna come up in my spot and disrespect me?"

Whack!

I grab Zoey by the waist and drag her off. "Baby, chill. Baby, chill. Let her go. Let her go."

Tonya struggles back to her feet and launches toward Zoey, but I plant my body between them and receive most of the blows coming from both sides. I've been in my fair share of fights but nothing compares to this catfight.

"Goddamn it, chill the fuck out," I roar. It takes some work, but I manage to get Zoey to sit her ass down while I drag Tonya back toward the damn door.

"Nah, nah," Zoey screams, picking up the phone. "She wants someone to press charges, tell her ass to stay right the fuck there."

Now, the hallway is crowded with people. In Bentley Manor everybody wants to know your business. A coupla kids grabbed Tonya's fake ponytail from the floor and were now twirling it around like a helicopter above their heads.

"Fuck that fat bitch," Tonya screams. "I don't know what the fuck you see in her anyway."

"Tonya, get the hell on. I ain't playing with you."

Finally I get her out the door and then slam the mutherfucker in her face. I lock it seconds before she starts twisting the doorknob.

I release an exhausted breath and look over at Zoey as she slams the phone down and starts pacing the floor like a caged animal.

"Are you all right, baby?" I ask, approaching. I know damn well she ain't. "Don't let that girl get to you."

"I can't stand that bitch. Why the hell did you have her up in my apartment?"

"She just showed up. Just calm down."

"Don't tell me to fucking calm down. How the hell are you going to let her disrespect me like that?"

"Baby, what would you have me do—hit her? Catch another case? You want me to go back to jail because of her crazy ass?"

She starts pacing faster. "Why the fuck did you have to knock her up?"

I shut the fuck up because we're now in a territory where there's no right or wrong answer. "Come here, baby." I pull her stiff body into my arms. "It's all right, calm down." I kiss the top her head. "She just said all that shit to get a rise out of you."

Zoey takes a couple of deep breaths before she starts to relax.

"Don't let her stress you. We're going to get through this. All right?" When she doesn't answer, I prompt her again. "All right?" I pull away so I can look down into her tear-streaked face. I wipe a few tears away with the pads of my thumbs. "We knew this wasn't going be easy when I got out. We're going to work through this . . . together. I got your back, you got mine. You're my ride-or-die chick, right? You're my Bonnie."

Finally, a smile flutters across her face, causing her cheeks to form perfect circles. "And you're my Clyde."

I kiss the top of her head and then work my way to her soft lips. I hope it repairs some of the damage Tonya has caused. "I know this is a bad time, but I need to borrow the car keys. I need to get over to my new p.o.'s office. I missed an appointment this morning."

She sighs, but scoops the car keys out of her pants pocket and hands them over. She also presses a twenty into my hand. "Put some gas in it. It's running low."

I stare at that twenty, feeling another layer of my manhood being stripped away. I can't even afford to put gas in her car. What the hell is she doing with me?

"Are you comin' straight back? I can put dinner on."

I nod. "Yeah." I force on a smile, kiss her forehead again, and head out the door.

I make it to my parole officer's office at precisely five o'clock. I'm hoping like hell that Ms. Harding is still here. I don't know what I'll do if I have to go back to prison over some simple fuckup like getting my days messed up.

I breathe a sigh of relief when I push on the door and it opens.

Marsha Harding, a husky five foot eight with a bleached-blond, half-inch Afro, strikes me as a dyke who'd yet to come out of the closet, glances up from behind the desk and then hangs up the phone. "You're late," she snaps.

"I know. I'm—"

"Up against the wall and place your hands above your head," she barks, like a military commander.

"Ms. Hard—"

"Do it!"

My hands clench at my side, a homicidal rage boils just below the surface. *Breathe, Demarcus. Breathe.*

Harding arched a furry brow. "Don't tell me you're one of the stupid ones."

Slowly, I turn and place my hands up against the wall.

"You know I can have your ass hauled back out to Jesup right now, don't you?" She approached, kicking my legs apart and then patting me down. "You were supposed to be here at ten a.m."

"I got my days mixed up. Thought it was tomorrow," I clip out. Her hands lingered in between my legs.

"Uh-huh. Mr. Jones, I run a tight ship around here. I ain't got a lot of time to be fertilizing your bullshit." A pair of handcuffs appears out of nowhere and clicks around my wrists.

Great! Just fucking great!

Beads of sweat pop up along my brow as a vision of this chick marching my ass to Jesup crowd my mind.

"Have you smoked or ingested any drugs?" she asks.

"No," I growl.

"You know you were also scheduled for a piss test this morning, right?"

"I'm clean."

"Uh-huh." She turns away and storms back over to her desk and picks up the phone.

"What the fuck? Who are you calling?" I turn from the wall.

"Like I said, you missed your appointment. That's a parole violation."

"Fuck! Don't do this shit to me. I've been busting my ass looking for a job. I just got my days mixed up."

She stops dialing.

"C'mon. Cut me some slack."

"I'm not in the slack-cutting business, Mr. Jones. Your circumstances are no different than the other parolees I have to keep tabs on. We have rules for a reason. Rules that *everyone* has to abide by."

I sense that she's wavering. "I know . . . and I'm sorry." *Just please hang up the phone.*

For an odd moment I see a spark of interest light her eyes when her gaze flickers across my body, but then disappears just as quickly, and the hard-nosed parole officer routine comes back in full force. Before I know it, I'm saying something I only halfway mean.

"Look, there's gotta be something I can do to convince you to give me another chance."

Harding's heavy brows climb to the center of her forehead. I've piqued her interest. For a long while our gazes lock.

Finally, she hangs up the phone and moves over to the door, closes and locks it. "I think I might be . . . persuaded to cut you a *little* slack."

Harding moves close to me and places a hand against my shoulder. "But my generosity deserves something in return."

The air in the room thickens and there's no point in me pretending not to know what she's talking about. The only question is whether I'm willing to pay her price.

She's waiting for some type of answer and it seems like forever for me to decide.

"Of course, if you want to go back to jail . . ." She returns to her desk and picks up the phone.

"No!" I bark and then soften it with a smile. "I mean, I'll be more than willing to thank you for your . . . generosity."

Harding hangs up; a wide smile stretches across her face. "I hoped you'd say that."

She produces the keys for the handcuffs and then removes them from my wrists. "Unbutton my blouse," she commands.

I hesitate.

"Well?"

Feeling another layer of my manhood being stripped from me, I force on a smile and do as I'm ordered.

Harding has an oddly shaped body where she has more gut than she has butt. I'm not turned on in the slightest. This is definitely one of those times where a man has to do what a man has to do—especially if he wants to keep his freedom. That's the reasoning I use as I set Harding on the edge of her desk and work the thick head of my cock into her fat pussy.

13

The Dealer

He's my son. Not Paco Taco, that motherfucker she was fucking, but mine. There is no denying this Maury Povich reveal moment as I read the results again. I've read this paper must be a hundred damn times since I got it in the mail today. I've been sitting on pins and needles the last two weeks waiting to find out if I had a baby with a junkie.

My parents gonna flip the fuck out.

Quilla ass is playing it cool and shit but I know she praying that the baby—Dashon—isn't mine.

Candy. *Humph.* I got her tricking ass holed up at Bentley Manor while I have the baby—*my* baby—with me. I've had him with me since that day in front of Circle K. This bitch didn't have no problem at all when I told her I was taking him. Matter of fact she had the nerve to tell me "Good, because I done had my turn for the last three months."

And me. What the fuck do I feel? That first day she dropped that load on me I was just numb as hell. But each day and night I kept him, washed him, fed him, and just held him. I fell for that little nigga. I'm glad that he's mine but eighteen years of dealing with Candy is a hard pill to fucking swallow.

I shift my eyes to the rearview mirror and look at him sitting in his car seat in the backseat. He's sleeping. My son. My seed. My legacy.

I got to do what the fuck I got to do.

I hop out of the SUV and open the back door to unlatch the car seat and pick up the carrier holding the baby. As I close the door with my hip, I make sure to put on my alarm. A nigga wasn't even trying to get got. Bentley Manor could be gutter as hell sometimes.

Did I think somebody would actually fuck with my ride especially with a gazillion people hanging out front? No. Am I taking any chances? Hell to the naw. Sometimes in the hood, people lived by "see and don't see"—especially when it comes to anything involving the police.

I'm glad as hell to walk into the stairwell and get out that August heat. Just them few steps from my truck to the building got sweat dripping down my back. When it's damn near a hundred degrees like today I leave the jewelry home. It's too hot for all that shit. If I was bulked up like 50 Cent my ass would come out of this wifebeater. That's just how hot it is.

I cover my son's face lightly with his blanket to keep him from inhaling in the scent of piss and the leftover scent of sweaty bodies. Even though I enjoy the hood, I never understand people using their hallways and the sides of their buildings for a damned toilet. I know it ain't everyone but even one motherfucker shitting on the wall is plenty.

I had Candy set up in this apartment I keep in Bentley Manor. Olive, this legit lady that I trust like crazy, has the apartment in her name. She only shows up when necessary to keep the apartment managers in the dark.

As I walk up the hall, I hear music thumping against the walls. "What the fuck going on in here?"

I put my key in the lock, but before I can turn the key the door opens and two young bucks walk out the apartment. They couldn't be no more than fourteen or fifteen.

I sit the baby's carrier down and grab one by the arm. "What the fuck was y'all doing in there?" I ask him, my face filled with anger.

They look at each other and I can see they nervous as shit. "We ain't the only ones," one of them says, his diamond earring so big and cloudy that it got to be fake.

"Hold up one sec." I pat them both down real quick to make sure they don't got shit of mine in their pockets before I push them the fuck on their way.

I grab up the baby carrier, pulling back his baby cover to check on him real quick. He smiles up at me and my fucking heart tugs like he has a string tied around it. Not sure what the fuck is going on in the apartment, I turn and knock on the scratched metal door of the apartment across the hall.

"Who?" a female yells through the door.

"This Kaseem."

I hear about ten fucking locks get undone and then the door swings open. "Whaddup, Lola. Your man home?"

She gives me a look that reminds me she don't play. Lola is a bad bitch. Her skin is dark as midnight without a bump in sight and her body is all about her flat stomach and ghetto ass. With her looks and that ass niggas is always trying to get at her, but she loyal as fuck to her man. I mean to the point of cussing a motherfucker out for even *thinking* she would fuck around on her man.

"I wanted you to watch my son while I see what the fuck going on over there." I nod my head back across the hall.

Lola looks over my shoulder and then rolls her eyes. "That's trick central. *That's* what the fuck goin' on. So please know when you see that dotted up eye on that trick that I had to check your bitch for trying to step to my man. You better let her know I don't play."

Oh shit. And Lola wasn't lying. I seen her beat a grown-ass man one time. She had that fool begging her to leave him the fuck be.

She took the carrier from me. "I ain't know you had a son, Kas," she says.

"Shit, neither did I."

"Well, I got him, so go handle your business."

She turns and I ain't gone lie that my eyes dipped right to that ass. Them gray sweatpants she got on isn't doing shit for hiding that up and down bounce. Okay, I know I said I got enough pussy to last me, but the fact that that ass look like it do *and* that she keep that pussy on lock the way that she do, make me want to nut all over her ass even more.

As soon as the door swings close, I turn and cross the hall to walk into my apartment.

The black-on-black decorated living room is empty, but as soon as I step to the hall I see three more teenage boys standing outside the bedroom door. One of these looks about twelve or thirteen. They eyes get big as shit seeing me and it don't take nothing but a hand motion for them to scramble out of there.

I open the bedroom door and one teenage is feeding his dick into Candy's mouth while another older guy is steadily pumping away in her pussy doggy-style on the edge of the bed.

Shit, I ain't mad she fucking niggas or even that she letting these young bucks run a train on her. Her crackhead ass is dead wrong to be handling her little pussy business on my thousand-dollar sheets. "Get the fuck out," I tell them, sounding aggravated as hell.

The old man jumps off her ass so quick that he trips over his pants and falls on his back with his Viagra hard-on pointing to the damn ceiling. I rush over and grab him up by the neck being sure to not let his wet dick touch my threads as I toss him headfirst into the hall.

While the fellas get the fuck out Candy just wipes spit and cum from her mouth while she lays back on the middle of the bed looking like a skeleton spray-painted brown.

I gave her somewhere to stay. Babysat before I even knew the baby was mine. Offered her rehab—which she refused. Gave her money. Food. Clothes. Everything but the dope she needed. Guess the bitch found her own way to make it happen. It's time to bring this circus to an end.

"You been smoking?"

"Not yet."

"Cover up."

Candy smiles and then spreads her legs showing me the hairiest pussy I ever seen in my life. "Wanna ride for old times' sake?"

"Naw, I'm good." Please. I wouldn't fuck Candy with a dildo.

I reach for the papers from the back pocket of my Tommy plaid shorts and fling them at her. "The results came back and the baby is mine."

She looks smug and shit. "I told you that."

"Those are papers giving me custody of our son. Sign them and then pack your shit because you outta here."

She rolls over onto her stomach and reaches for a pack

of Newports on the nightstand. Her poor little ass looks sunken in as she lights a cigarette. "Where my money?" she asks.

I reach in my front pocket for a wad of money rolled together and held with a rubber band.

"Throw in a cookie and I'm out." A cookie is the flat and round weight of crack. She looks me dead in the eye when she says it, too. I just want her gone. This bitch is selling my son to me for dope and money and she hasn't once called to check on him or even ask me as I stand here how he doing.

She gots to go.

"Deal."

"What's wrong, Daddy? You don't like?"

I look up at Suga standing in front of me in nothing but a pair of heels, a thong, and a smile. She trying her best to get me focused but my mind is somewhere else.

As soon as I dropped Candy's no-good, scandalous ass to the train station—without even asking her where the fuck she going—I headed straight out to the country where me and Usher rented a three-bedroom brick house in Olive's name. We call it the Trick Set. Not too many people know about the house. They might have heard about it but they don't know where it is. Quilla was completely clueless about the Trick Set. Shee-it. It's at this spot that we did all our dirt. Cut up drugs. Stash weight. Trick. Party. Crash. Whateva.

Right now a lot of our upper level crew is just chilling, watching TV, playing video games, smoking, and drinking. Usher is in one of the three bedrooms with some chick named Viesha that he met at Visions last week.

Earlier tonight I planned to chill with Quilla at her town house but when I called her she was at the mall with her cousins. Of course she was first on my list, but when I have some free time to spend with someone, I always go to my second string. Right now the twins were giving Quilla a run for my money. Fuck it. I was down for twice the pussy and twice the fun so I gave them a call to meet me here. Suga was home and Spyce was out, so now Suga is out here with me.

Even though we were still alone in the master bedroom my mind was on my son. I paid Lola a bill to watch him for me, but really my ass is ready to kiss Suga good night and jet. I'm sick of the smell of weed and liquor coming through the closed door. Sick of the company. Sick of the game. The hustle. I'm not even in the mood to fuck no more. She's swinging her big titties against my face and my dick ain't jumped to life yet.

I reach behind her to slap her ass. "I got a lot on my mind. Do me a favor and head back home."

She squats down in front of me until her pussy looks like a fist in her thong. When she starts working her hip in a slow grind she uses her hands to lift up her titties to tease her own hard nipples with her tongue. "I ain't gone lie, Daddy. I want that dick and bad, too," she tells me, her accent a mix of hood and Down South charm—sexy as fuck. "You ain't got to do shit, Daddy, but let me take care of that dick. Watch."

My heart and my mind tell me I'm ready to go, but my dick stands at attention and now *it's* ready to get wet.

"I don't have much time," I tell her as I raise my hips and work my vintage Gucci jeans down.

Suga laughs as she stands up. She lets her tits go free and they bounce and jiggle as they land back against her chest. With a wicked-ass smile, this sexy bitch pulls her thong to the side before she climbs on my lap. "You know damn well this pussy right here don't need much time to make that dick do what it do. Do it?"

"Hell, naw." I close my eyes and let my head fall back against the back of the chair as she slides down on my dick and starts a slow grind that doesn't stop until I am gripping her hips and fucking back as I cum like there is no tomorrow.

Hours later, I look down at my son lying asleep in my arms as I stand at the bay windows of my apartment. *Everything* is different now. Everything.

I'm tired.

Not sleepy tired, but fed up. Ready for something new. Tired of the lies. The double life. The secrets. The life.

I ease him onto my bare shoulder and I'm glad I left the Set, picked him up, and came home. Just me and my son. It isn't about just me anymore. It can't be.

I press a kiss to his cheek before I look out at the Atlanta night skyline. My city. My streets. My hell.

Things *have to* change.

14

The Playa

Ain't nothing worse than bein' broke except bein' broke without a way to get my hands on more money. I don't know why I'm standin' here lookin' in this empty-ass fridge. Ain't shit I can make happen with the dried crust of some shit I spilled weeks ago and an empty cereal box.

"Man, this 'bout a bunch of bullshit." I slam the door so hard that the little-ass fridge leans with it and rocks with it.

Two months since Shaterica's ass copped to that murder for me. I'm behind on the fifty dollars a month rent. I can't drive the car 'cause I ain't even had no gas money. Shit, over three dollars a gallon? My ass ain't drivin' no damn where. I'm feenin' for a fucking cigarette and a blunt in this bitch and if I didn't get somethin' in my stomach soon this motherfucker gonna collapse.

I'd have some loot if that tricky bitch Shay didn't run

off with the money I made off them fake-ass purses. I woke up one morning with my dick *and* my pockets drained. If I see that little bitch again I'm gonna choke her ass the fuck out. Period.

On top of that my other bitches tryna act brand new on a nigga. Fuck 'em. All I need is a new set but I got to get my head back in the game. That murder fuckin' wit my ass big-time. Sometimes I wake up at night all sweaty and shit after dreamin' 'bout the night I killed that fool. I can't let that shit get at me. I took care of keepin' my ass out of jail. It's all over. I just got to get my head back in the game.

I see a mouse shoot across the floor and into a small hole in the corner of the kitchen. His ass gots to be goin' to get somethin' to eat 'cause there ain't even a crumb up in this bitch.

I walk my ass out the kitchen on top of the dirty clothes and papers on the floor. I grab a wifebeater that used to be white and slide it on as I head down the hall. I don't stop 'til I leave that junky-ass apartment behind. As soon as that metal door slams behind me I freeze, scared that Polette stalkin'-ass 'bout to flash me again.

She probably drunk as hell. Good 'cause I ain't in the mood for her shit.

It's about twelve and already the hall is filled with the sounds of music and TVs blaring, kids laughing or crying. It ain't never quiet around this place. Never. Somebody's ass is always awake and makin' some kinda noise. Thank

God August is almost over so these badass kids can get they sickenin' asses back in school.

As soon as I jog down the stairs and outside the building, Miz Cleo and Miz Osceola walk up to me. I step to the left to walk past they ass. Jane Pittman and Harriet Tubman step to the left and block me. I step to the right. Here they go with the same damn thing.

"Something in the milk ain't clean, Cleo," Miz Osceola says as she leans on her bat like it's a cane.

Miz Cleo shakes her hand to make the ice cubes in her jelly jar of ice water rattle. "It sure ain't."

"People 'round here best remember that what's done in the dark always come to the light. Ain't that right, Cleo?"

She takes a deep sip of her water and smacks her lips before she answers. "Sure is."

Do they know about Shay? What the fuck is they gettin' at?

"Are y'all talkin' to me?" I ask, crossing my arms over my chest.

Miz Osceola sticks her bat under her arm. For a second I think she 'bout to hit me. I don't put shit past these old birds.

"I ain't got but one word for you . . . karma." She looks me up and down like shit on a new pair of shoes.

"It's a bitch," Miz Cleo adds the fuck on as she rattles that ice again.

"Yo, man, what the fuck ever." I push right between them and keep on steppin' from the nosy asses. One of these days somebody gonna make them mind they damn business. Them birds thought they owned Bentley Manor and had they hands and they noses in every fuckin' thing that went down in this bitch.

Humph. Maybe if Miz Cleo had swept in front of her own door her ass woulda known her granddaughter was fuckin' that preacher last winter. And from what I heard a fuckin' girl was livin' right up in this bitch as a dude and lot of people didn't even know about *that* shit—until her ass shot and killed her lover's husband.

They better stay the fuck outta my shit. That I know for sho. They probably mad 'cause word out that I was fuckin' other chicks while Shaterica ass doin' time, but fuck that she got ten years? Who the fuck thought my dick wasn't gonna get wet in ten years? Shee-it. That's a bunch of bullshit for real.

Plus, Shaterica ass is long gone. Sentenced. Done deal. I done moved the fuck on and Shaterica and everybody else might as well do the same. Fuck it. Life is too short.

I head to the Circle K to lift some detergent and see if any of my friends hangin' around for me to borrow some money. If I want some more bitches on my roll I had to get some clothes washed, get a haircut, and get my shit back together. One of the main rules in getting' what you need from a chick is to not look like you need it. Stupid, right? But so true.

I'm halfway down the block when I see Pop-Pop and Rollo walking toward me pushing some dude in a wheelchair. These two old dudes let drugs and alcohol fuck them up major—that's why I don't fuck with nothin' stronger than weed and Budweisers. I don't want to wind up like they ass downtown or in front of any corner with a store beggin' for spare change.

The closer we all get to each other the more I got my eyes on the man in the wheelchair. Who the fuck is that? His head bobbin' like a motherfucker. "Whaddup, Pop-Pop. Rollo."

"Hey, young blood. You know where a check cashing place at?" Rollo asks, his hands ashy and tight as fuck on the handles of the wheelchair.

I squint my eyes to keep out some of the sun beaming down on us. "Just the ones over on Piedmont."

"That's a long walk. You don't think he gone start to stink, is it?" Pop-Pop asks Rollo.

"I don't guess so."

Stink?

I bend down and put my hand on the man in the wheelchair and it's stiff. Dead stiff.

Listen. I been a hustler a long damn time and it don't take me long to figure out two and two together to get four. "I know y'all silly asses ain't trying to cash *his* check?"

These gray-hair Grady-looking fools from *Sanford and Son* both look at me scared as shit. I look back at these fools like they stupid.

"What?" Rollo asks, his grip back tight on the handles. "We found him dead in his room. Nobody know he dead yet. His check just sittin' there. We got his IDs. We got him. Our friend wouldn't want his money to go to waste like that."

"Damn straight," Pop-Pop adds.

Humph. Crazy shit like this always goin' down in the hood. Where else would somebody feel free to roll around with a dead body? Man, let me get the fuck from these fools 'fore the cops roll me with they ass.

One thing this little run-in taught me is to make it in the hood you gotta do what you gotta do. Fuck it.

I turn and walk back to Bentley Manor. Sweat drippin' down my chest and nuts but I didn't break my stride one damn bit. Man, fuck the dumb shit. I'm sick of being hungry. Sick of bein' broke. Sick of not havin' more bitches than I can fuck in a week. Sick of playin' this fuckin' marry-me game with Shaterica so that she keep her ass in jail.

I'm sick of all this shit. It's time for a nigga like me to get back on top and to do what my ass needed to find a backbone to replace Shaterica.

I gots to do what the fuck I gotta do . . . for now.

I run up the stairs and down the hall. I knock before I change my mind. The door opens. Polette sees me and smiles like she won the lottery.

"Welcome home, lover," she slurs, already unzipping her dingy robe and letting it fall to the floor.

Damn. Life is a bald-headed, no-good, raggedy-mouth, stink-pussy bitch.

15

The Pimp

Fuck it.

I'm a nice man, but from time to time, I have to beat a bitch down. The success of any business centers on the quality of his product: pussy, in my case. Good pussy. Clean and drug-free pussy. After all, any nigga can get a crackhead ho to suck his dick for $20. My rates are $3,500 an hour with a three-hour minimum. Cash only. So when I get a call from a disgruntled but longtime client demanding his money back because one of my girls are so high and fucked up that he can't even get his dick hard, well, then it's time for me to put my foot down on a bitch's neck.

But then when I learn that same bitch is tryna play snitch, I gotta take things to another level.

Sabrina has been working for me for close to ten years, so it ain't like she doesn't know the fuckin' deal. She ain't stupid, slow, or hooked on muthafuckin' phonics either. So while she's sobbin' in front of me about how sorry she is, I don't fuckin' want to hear it.

"You're a fuckin' disappointment, Sabrina," I say as I walk a circle around her standing nude body. It's a fuckin' hot body too. Five-eight, slim, with a red beans and rice booty. Three years ago, she was one of my top moneymakers. Now I only get a request for her services once maybe twice a month. The bitch has been seriously slipping.

This is what happens when you deal with sloppy bitches. I would have caught this shit sooner if I wasn't constantly dealing with Corrine's bullshit. The girl has run away from home twice. Each time, she showed up at my momma's apartment.

First time I've heard of anyone wanting to run *to* Bentley Manor.

"C'mon, Sweet. I'm sorry," Sabrina says; her voice cracking. "You know me. I was just having a bad night."

"A bad night?" I laugh. "Client says you were so high you fell asleep and pissed the bed. Call me crazy, but that sounds like more than a bad night."

She whimpers a bit, avoids meeting my eyes.

"So whatcha smokin', huh? Crack? Meth? I'm sure the shit is stronger than weed if you're pissing the bed."

Sabrina doesn't answer. She just stands there looking straight ahead with tears streaking down her face. Like I give a fuck. "Whatcha cryin' for?" I unbutton my jacket and hand it to Fat Joe.

"I'm sooo sorry, Sweet," she sobs, trembling like a leaf. "I promise it won't happen again."

"Oh, I know the shit ain't gonna happen again," I tell her. "No bitch fucks with my money."

Another sob.

"What the fuck you cryin' for?" I bark. "Ain't I always been good to you?"

Silence.

"What—I ain't been good to you? Is that what you tryna say?"

The crying bitch shakes her head. "You've always been good to me. Always."

"So why you fuck me, huh? You cost me fourteen large. Now what am I supposed to do about that?" I roll up my sleeves.

"Sweet, I swear, I'll get you your money."

"How? By fucking someone else? You think another client wants to fuck a crackhead for fourteen K? What fuckin' fantasy world you livin' in?" I move in close, notice the subtle swell of her nose. "Oh, you're a snortin' bitch," I accuse and before she has a chance to answer I coldcock her ass dead in the nose and watch her ass smack the floor. "Get yo ass back up," I growl. When she takes too long I completely lose it and begin wailing on her.

Let's keep it real, I don't force these bitches to work for me. They're free to come and go as they please. But when they are on the fuckin' clock, sportin' that tattooed diamond, I expect nuthin' less than their A game.

Instead of taking this beat-down that she's due, Sabrina dumb ass starts hurlin' threats at me.

"Fuck you," she spats, still trying to cup the blood shooting out of her nose as she squirms away. "You ain't shit."

"Oh, I ain't shit, huh?" I sock her dead in her mouth and watch in satisfaction when she spits out a few teeth. "Your ass must be high right now. Is that it?"

"You're gonna get yours, muthafucka. You gonna get yours!"

"Bitch, please. You mean that deal you tried to strike this morning when you were arrested for drug possession?"

She stops squirming to stare at me.

"What? You don't think I have my eyes and ears every- where? You thought you were just goin' to serve me up and you walk or some shit? Yeah. Your ass has been smokin' the good shit." I turn to Fat Joe. "You still got that big Bowie knife I got you for Christmas?"

Fat Joe's evil smile hooked the corners of his lips. "Yes, sir." He reaches into his coat pocket. "I never leave home without it."

Sabrina starts squirming again. "What are you 'bout to do?"

"I'm about to make myself a drink," I tell her. "Fat Joe, here, is going to get me those beautiful double Ds I paid for."

Her hands fall away from her busted face to cover her chest. "Nooo."

"You didn't think you were going to keep those mutha-fuckas, did you?"

Now the bitch can move. She's on her feet and rushing toward the door like that damn cartoon Speedy Gonzales. I guess she was just going to haul off naked down the street. But while fumbling with the lock, Fat Joe catches up with her and snatches her by her long hair. At least that's real.

Sabrina screams.

I laugh. "Fuck me, huh? Fuck you!" My cell phone rings. I scoop it out of my pocket and see my home phone number across the screen. I answer the call. "Yeah, what is it?"

A pause and then Renee says, "Who's that scream-ing?"

"I'm working," I say and then glance at my watch. "Wait." I glance up at Fat Joe. "Take care of that bitch in the bathroom and then clean this shit up. I'll send the car back for you."

"Wait. No, Sweet. I'm sorry," Sabrina screams and sobs. "Please let me make it up to you. Sweet, please."

I roll my eyes at that shit. "Erase that bitch," I tell Fat Joe, grab my jacket and cane, and head out the door of the high-rise condominium.

"Sweet, are you there?" Renee screeches in my ear.

"Calm the fuck down, Renee." I swear I don't know how much more of her mouth I can stand. The pussy is good, but goddamn. "What is the damn emergency?"

"Don't snap at me, Sweet. I'm not in the fuckin' mood."

"What the fuck?" I pull the phone away from my ear and stare at it as I head toward the Bentley. When I place the muthafucka back against my ear, she finally tells me the deal.

"The school called," she says. "*Your daughter* has gotten into trouble and they want to see you."

She hangs up before I can question her further. "Shit."

"How the fuck someone get in trouble on the first day of school?" I bark at Destiny as we head out to the suburbs and Corrine's new school in white suburbia. It's a rare day that he's dressed like a man in casual jeans and a Sean John T-shirt.

I'm already dreading what the fuck I'll hear once I get to the school. I'm doubly annoyed that this little girl is costing me time and, therefore, money.

I called Renee back and tried to get her to run up to the school but all she did was laugh and hang up on me. Wait 'til I see her ass when I get home. Is it too much to ask for a little help with Corrine? What the hell do I know about raising girls?

"Calm down," Destiny says. "You shoulda known that there would be an adjustment period."

I groan.

When the Bentley pulls up to Alpharetta High School's half-empty parking lot, I can't believe my stomach is actually twisted into knots. Is this what the hell kids do to you?

Sure, in the ten weeks Corrine has crashed at my crib, I haven't had the chance to get to know her, but cut me some slack. The girl rarely talks. She just eats my food and spends my money. Fuck. The only person she talks to is Destiny.

Frankly, I think I'm doing good. I've cut back on the number of parties at the house, no more porn being produced at the crib, and all my working girls have been instructed to stay clear—well, except for Destiny . . . and Renee.

What it all boils down to is I don't know what the hell I'm doing. But if Corrine thinks that I'm going to be running up to this bitch every day, she better think again.

"You want me to come in with you?" Destiny asks.

"Nah. I got this. Wait here."

I make my way to the principal's office rather easily and when I see Corrine sitting in the chair, she has the good sense to look away and drop her head. I take the seat next to her and glance over. "You want to tell me what all this is about?"

Before Corrine can answer, the principal walks into the office. She's an attractive midforties bookworm type in a casual brown pants suit with a respectable length of hair weaved into her head.

"You must be Mr. Johnson," she says, beaming at me

and pushing her glasses up her nose before offering me her hand.

I accept it with a broad smile. "Correct. And you must be the principal."

"Principal O'Grady," she says and then releases my hand to make her way over to her desk. "Thank you for coming, Mr. Johnson."

I make another glance over at Corrine and notice her head is still tucked low. "No trouble at all," I lie and return to my chair. "What seems to be the problem?"

Ms. O'Grady takes a deep breath and I catch a flicker of disappointment in her brown eyes. Not a good sign.

"The reason I called you here, Mr. Johnson, was because your daughter was caught in the boys' bathroom performing a strip show."

I lean forward in my chair. "Come again?" I then look over at Corrine, who still refuses to look at me.

Ms. O'Grady leans over her desk and carefully braids her fingers together. "I'm sorry, Mr. Johnson, we can't allow this sort of behavior at this school."

I know it's hypocritical of me, given all the shit I've done—hell, the shit I'd done when I was Corrine's age, but I'm suddenly flushed with embarrassment and shame. Meanwhile, I sense the principal is waiting for me to say or do something. "I see," is all I can think to say.

Misreading my silence, Ms. O'Grady jumps in as an attempt to help me out of this sticky situation. "I know this sort of thing can be upsetting," she begins. "And while I certainly don't condone what has happened this afternoon, I must stress to you that girls Corrine's age are very impressionable. With today's media glorifying the bad behavior of rap and movie stars, young ladies are receiving the wrong messages. It's my understanding that Corrine hasn't been under your care long. Is there a positive woman figure in Corrine's life?"

"Well, there's my wife. Her stepmother."

Corrine breaks her silence to bark out a laugh.

I place my hand on her arm and signal for her to shut the fuck up.

"Well, maybe she can help. Give her guidance in what is appropriate behavior for a young lady."

"Of course," I say, mainly because there isn't anything else to say. This whole situation has thrown me off my game. "We will certainly talk to Corrine when we get home," I say, standing. I don't want to stay in this office another second.

"Corrine." My tone makes it clear that it's time to go. I then return my attention to Ms. O'Grady. "Thank you for your time and for bringing this to my attention."

"Unfortunately, Mr. Johnson, I'm going to have to suspend Corrine for two weeks, but I surely hope that you and your wife can resolve this matter and we won't have to have this conversation again."

"Thank you for your time," I repeat. I move to the desk and stretch my hand across it. We shake and then

I lead Corrine out of the office. It isn't until we're finally back outside do I take in a deep breath, but my irritation remains.

"Destiny, ride up front with Anderson. I'd like to talk privately with my daughter."

Corrine's eyes widen. "Damn. You clean up good," she says to Destiny.

"Don't hate." He smiles back at her.

In the car, we roll in silence for a few minutes. I have no idea what to say or how to address this issue. One thing is clear, I have to say something. "What the fuck were you thinking?"

Corrine stares out of the window.

"Girl, don't make me repeat myself."

Corrine jerks her head toward me. "I was making money."

There's something about staring into eyes that look like mine that unnerves me, something about the determined set of her chin and her aloof attitude that saddens me. All my life, I've been a smooth-talking pimp. I can sell Donald Trump oceanfront property in Arizona.

Now, twice in the last hour I've been rendered speechless. For the first time since Corrine has moved in with me, I wonder about what her childhood has been like up until this point.

I mean *really* wondered.

For me and my crew, I know why we're fucked up and always chasing the mighty dollar. I hustled pussy out of

Bentley Manor until I made something out of my life. What else could I have done? I don't have any other talents to speak of. I'm not a rapper or a ballplayer. And I damn sure wasn't a Cosby kid, where college was ever *really* an option.

But Corrine?

Hell, I haven't even asked her why her momma dropped her off. I have no idea what her short fifteen years on this earth has been like. Damn, I could've reached out to the girl a little better than I have.

During our combative stares, I'm the first to turn away and glance back out of the window.

"Money ain't everything," I say, surprising myself.

"Yeah, right, said the pimp to the ho."

I glance at her again, idly wondering about my daughter's sexuality. "You turning tricks?"

"Why? You want to pimp me out like you do my grandma?"

"What?"

"I heard you asking her for your money when you picked me up at her place that day." Corrine's eyes rake over me with disgust. "What kind of man pimps out his own mother?"

I laugh in her face.

"What—that's funny to you?"

"Yeah. Since my mother doesn't pay me a dime," I say, rolling my eyes. "Look, growing up, me and my brother would take her trick money to make sure there was groceries in the apartment. But . . . that was a very long time ago."

"But I heard you."

"That's just a routine we go through. A joke. I show up at Bentley Manor once a month to check in on her, make sure she's taking her medicine and has food in her place. That's all."

She studies me as if trying to decide if she believes me.

I see a girl who is fifteen going on fifty.

"Look." I lick my lips. "I know we haven't exactly taken the time to get to know each other."

"Save it," she says, turning back toward the window. "You and my *new mommy* have made it perfectly clear that I'm not wanted. That's why I gotta hustle up a few dollars of my own to get the hell out of there. I don't want to make it habit to stay where I'm not wanted."

"I never said that I didn't want you."

"Actions speak louder than words."

I'm determined to make my point. "If I didn't want you in my house, you wouldn't be there. Believe that. It's just . . ." I straighten my shoulders and I struggle for the right words. "Look. You gotta cut me some slack. I don't know what the fuck I'm doing. Being a father wasn't supposed to be in the cards from me. I never knew you existed."

"Well, I do. Now what?" She swivels her neck back toward me.

Hell, were Renee and I really twelve, three years

younger than Corrine, when we hooked up? When I start thinking about the freaking things we did, it makes me wonder what right I had telling my daughter what to do or not do.

I look at her—a face so much like mine—and realize I don't want her to travel down the same road I did. I grew up where food was scarce in a small, rat- and cockroach-infested apartment. I was hard because life had been hard on me. It doesn't have to be that way for my daughter.

I take a good look at her outfit: short, short skirt, tight shirt, and a few more curves than she had just two months ago. "You dress like a hooker," I say absently.

"I'm just showing my support for the family business."

"I'm trying to talk to you," I say on a more reasonable voice than I felt. "I know I haven't been the best father figure toward you and I . . . apologize."

No response.

"Corrine, look at me."

Time seems to stretch for forever, but I wait and finally she turns her head and meets my gaze.

"Why don't we just start over? I haven't done right by you. There's nothing we can do about the past, but we can work on the here and now."

Distrust lingers in her eyes and I can't blame her.

"In the morning I'm going to withdraw you from that school. You're going to a private school where we can get a fresh start."

"Fine. Whatever."

"And what do you say we go shopping? Anything you want—long as the clothes are . . . tasteful."

She doesn't answer but the slight change in her body language lets me know I've just said the right thing. Maybe I can turn this around, but just how does a pimp raise a lady?

16

The Killer

"In the name of God, the Merciful, the Compassionate. Say O Muhammad. He is God the One God, the Everlasting Refuge, who has not begotten, nor has been begotten, and equal to Him is not anyone," I recite chapter 112 of my heavily worn copy of the Quran.

The small group of teenagers surrounding me chuckles and laughs.

I lift my head and level my gaze with the leader of this pathetic gang of hoodrats. "What's so funny, my brotha?"

"You!" the boy snaps back and receives a round of laughter and a few dabs from his crew. "Man, you a muthafuckin' joke out here preachin' that shit. How you sound after servin' a dime for some bullshit?" The kid rolls his eyes. "Nigga, please."

"When one finds enlightenment, it's his duty to share his knowledge."

"Well, has your *enlightenment*," another kid jumps in, complete with air quotes, "helped you find a *job, nigga?*"

The kids laugh and a couple of them stroll off.

I grind my teeth together, not sure why today their blatant disrespect was riding my last nerve. I put up with much worse during lockdown. As I watch them walk away, I feel nothing but pity stir in the pit of my stomach. "The reason I'm out here," I tell the remaining few, "is to help you avoid the mistakes I've made."

Miz Cleo and Miz Osceola cackle from their stoop.

"Then you're gonna be out here all day," Miz Cleo says, chuckling, and then returns her attention to her great-grandbaby, who was trying her hand at climbing up on a tricycle.

"Whatever." One kid with perfectly lined cornrows and intense hazel-green eyes stares me down. "Ain't nobody wanna hear all that Allah shit. Next thing you know, you'll be out gettin' jacked for sellin' bean pies out in this muthafucka."

His lone buddy snickered.

"Besides. I'ma Christian and shit. I ain't down for blowin' my ass up for no damn body."

"You're talking about Muslim extremist groups," I tell them. "That's not what I'm preachin' to you."

"Whatever, nigga," my green-eyed monster says. "I heard your ass was a killah."

I tense.

"Whocha kill?"

"I didn't go to jail for killing anyone."

"Nah. You tried to kill your old lady, but I ain't talkin' 'bout that. The streets have been saying your shit was pretty tight. Knocked off a coupla niggas when you used to run with the Disciples."

I straighten my shoulders about as far back as I can. "Again. That's why I'm out here tryna talk some sense into you boys. The streets ain't got no love for you. It just uses you up and spits you back out. Drugs, money, violence. Been there, done that."

The boys just laugh in my face. "Nigga, you done got soft," the green-eyed boy laughs. "Aww, shit. There goes Sweet."

I turn my head and watch as a slick-ass Bentley rolls through the wrought-iron gates.

"That nigga's paid," one of the boys exclaimed with open admiration. "When I grow up, I'm gonna be a big-time pimp just like my man Sweet."

"I hear he has so many hos that his hos have hos."

The kids crack up again, but I remained rooted to my spot on the concrete, watching, with nearly the same admiration as the hoodrats standing beside me.

The driver pops out the vehicle first and then opens that back door. When Tavon Johnson climbs out, our eyes meet from across the way and my heart nearly stops. I'm trying like hell not to be sucked back into an old memory, but the shit is nearly impossible. Before I know it, I'm back in the old, black Cutlass, trying to lift a gun that's too heavy.

One shot.

Two shots.

I close my eyes. What would Tavon do if he knew that I was the one who'd killed his older brother?

"Damn, look at that suit," someone says, still admiring their old neighborhood pimp. "How much somethin' like that set a nigga back, you think?"

"Humph. Humph. Humph," Miz Cleo grunts behind us. "Damn shame. That boy is the last one you young'uns need to be tryna be like. Goin' down that road ain't nothin' but trouble."

"Sure you right," Miz Osceola cosigns. "What you boys need are daddies. Someone to guide you down the right path."

"Shoot." One of the kids folds his arms. "My momma says that she's both my momma and daddy. She says she don't need nobody help take care of me and my brothers."

"Boys *need* men," Miz Cleo retorts. "Good strong men to keep you in line."

That comment causes another ripple of laughter as well.

"Please. Momma says I'm the man of the house now."

I look down at the kid. He couldn't have been more than thirteen.

"I run shit in my crib. Hustlin' for Kaseem puts food on the table. Nowahmean?"

Miz Osceola snorts. "Girl, you just wastin' you breath.

These hardheaded boys don't want to learn nothin'. Just like Demarcus when he was their age."

I blink out of the old memories and turn to face the old ladies.

"What? Don't tell me you forgot how we used to try and talk some sense into you when you were their age?"

Shame creeps into my face. I lost track of how many times I used to tell them to mind their own damn business. Sometimes when I got too smart Miz Cleo would chase me with that same bat propped up against the door now.

"Jesus," I swear under my breath. "Does nothing change around here?"

"'Fraid not," Miz Cleo said solemnly. "'Fraid not."

When I glance around again, the teenagers have strolled off, talking and laughing at their own private jokes.

"So, are you really out here trying to make a change?" Miz Cleo asks.

I'm stunned she actually engaging into a conversation with me. "Trying."

The two old ladies stare me up and down but whether I pass their inspection or not remains to be seen.

"Well, I don't know if I believe all that Muslim stuff you be preachin', but these kids need some kind of guidance. Of course, I'm the last one to talk." Her gaze drifts back over to her excited great-granddaughter. "I haven't been back to church since her momma died."

"But you pray and talk to God every day," Miz Osceola reminds her.

Miz Cleo nods but sadness clings to the lines etched in her face.

"How long have you been living here, Miz Cleo?" I ask.

"So long sometimes I think I was born here," she says.

I suddenly have an image of me sitting on that stoop forty years from now, a Louisville slugger by my side, watching time tick by. I don't know how they do it.

Zoey steps out of our building, beaming a smile at me.

"Hey, Miss Zoey."

The teenagers have returned to gawk at my girl. She may be thick but every red-blooded male recognizes the power of the booty. And my baby has plenty of it.

"Hey, guys." Zoey waves to her fan club before walking over to me.

"What's up?"

"Do you mind runnin' to the store for some milk and eggs?"

"Sure. Not a problem," I say.

She stretches out her hand to give me her car keys and a folded twenty.

I automatically clench my jaw; my temper is on instant simmer. The last thing I want is for these kids to see this shit. How would it look for me to be out here trying to teach boys to be men when it's likely they have more money in their pockets than I do?

"I got it," I tell her, even though I'm mentally calculating the chump change in my pocket.

"Well, don't you want the car keys?" she asks.

"I'll walk."

She frowns. It's just like a woman not to understand a man's pride.

"I need the exercise," I add before she starts arguing. I turn and head down the cracked sidewalk with my Quran tucked safely under my arm. As I approach Sweet's smooth-ass ride, I can't help but imagine what it would be like to have my ass sitting in the backseat. Jealousy pricks my soul while my eyes bug out the closer I get. *This nigga rollin' like this?*

I stop next to his whip and catch the evil-eyed gaze from the chauffeur, tellin' me to keep it movin'.

I ignore his fat ass and check out the rims.

"Like what you see, honey?"

My eyes finally land on the beautiful woman in the backseat. She looks familiar.

"Well, well, well." Tavon's smooth voice floats out to me.

My head jerks up as I watch a ghost walk toward me. "Demarcus Jones. I ain't seen your ass around here in a hot minute."

"Just got out the pen," I tell him.

"Well, you sure are a big swollen mutherfucka. You been pumpin' iron behind bars?"

"Got to pass the time some kind of way."

He bobs his head as he continues to study me. "Well,

I could use a big man like you down at the club. Bounce some of the undesirables to the curb, that sort of thing." He reaches inside his jacket and withdraws a business card. "Give me a holler if you're ever looking for work."

"Thanks," I say, taking the card, but I have no intention of ever using it. "I'll keep it in mind."

17

The Dealer

Starting about a week ago, toward the end of August, a lot of my lower-level dealers started getting robbed for their money and drug stashes. At first the stickups seemed random, but soon it was hard to deny. Somebody was fucking with my business and fucking with my business meant they are fucking with my money.

I walked in the Trick Set earlier and found Usher and some nameless trick butt naked and tied to each other. Our entire stash gone—even down to the scales and the rest of the equipment we used to bag it all up. Wasn't shit to do but chalk it up to a loss, since we couldn't call the police.

Now everybody is back strong on that "protect ya neck" bullshit. From Usher all the way down, them fellas want to man up with guns around the clock like we a cartel or some shit. The more I tell them to chill, the hotter they get under their Polo collars.

They all speculating on this one and that one behind the robberies. Before you know it there will be some silly-ass war that is just what the politicians and the news media want. That makes black-on-black crime and the war on drugs always be at the top of the damn news. That shit brings the heat of the police into the hood and slows up business.

See, I *always* think of the bigger picture. I'm far from stupid.

A soft-ass play for my reign is the last thing I need right now. I have my people with their ears to the streets for anybody who knows what went down. I had to re-route two runs this week in case somebody was watching I95. Olive had already given notice on the rental, so for now that was the end of the Trick Set. On top of all that, Usher and me were running through the list of tits and dicks who knew how to get to the house. Somebody *had* to talk.

Now shit is getting mad complicated. I might be in the game and avoiding violence but that don't mean the next up-and-comer wouldn't do whatever whenever to get rid of me. Fuck that. I ain't trying to die to be the drug kingpin of the South. I have choices to make.

My bedroom door opens and I turn around as Quilla walks in holding Dashon in her arms. She looks good as hell holding my son. I know it had to hurt her to hold another woman's child for me—especially without kids of her own. This whole baby-out-the-blue situation hasn't been easy for Quilla to swallow, but she's taking it like a trouper. It helped that the baby was before her time and that Candy was long gone—no baby momma drama. Quilla wasn't going for that bullshit.

Every day she got closer and closer to my son, and just like his daddy he won Quilla's no-nonsense ass over. Ever since then she stepped right in and helped me. Every step of the way she was right there loving him and taking care of him just like me. His nursery. His clothes and supplies. Even being there when I first took him to my parents.

On the real? All of it makes me feel like I love her. I mean really love her.

After that bullshit that went down with Candy I really didn't want to be caught up in another woman. The more I pulled away from the game and toward her and the baby, the more I feel myself falling.

"He looks just like you, Kas," she tells me as she lays him down in the bassinet I keep in my bedroom. "I'm going to miss him while we in Puerto Rico."

She has on a pale yellow sheer nightgown that does nothing to cover up the matching teddy that hugs the curves of her body. I feel my dick stirring in my silk pajama bottoms but I don't want to fuck Quilla. It's her mind I'm after. Her thoughts. Her opinions. Is she gone ride or what? Is the money and the status of being my lady more important than me?

"I'm feeling like I want out lately."

Quilla looks over her shoulder at me as she unbends her body. "Out of what?" she asks with some attitude all up and through her shit. "Out of us? I know you not breakin' up—"

"Out of the game, Quilla."

Her whole expression changes. "Oh. Oh . . . okay. Soooo . . . what's up? What's going on?"

My cordless rings and I pick it up from the base. It's my moms. "Hey, Ma."

"I'm just making sure y'all still bringing our grandson."

I glance over at Quilla and I can tell her mind is filled up with my news. *What is she thinking right now?* "We're getting dressed right now. We should be to the house in an hour."

"Good."

The line goes quiet and I know what is coming next.

"Have you heard from his mother?"

My left eye twitches in irritation. "No, Ma. I told you she signed over custody to me and she moved out of state."

"What kind of mother doesn't want to see her child?"

Ever since I got back the test results I told my parents about Dashon and most of the situation with Candy. Why the hell I got to go through this shit every time we talk about my son? Fuck Candy. For real. "Ma, let me finish getting dressed or we gone miss our plane."

"See you in a bit."

I gladly hang up but as soon as I set the phone back on the base my Mogul PDA starts to ring. I don't miss Quilla throwing her hands up in the air before she walks into the bathroom.

"Whaddup, Ush?"

"I need to holler at you. You home?"

"Yeah, but I'm leaving in a few."

"Hit me up when you get back."

"That's Monday."

The line goes quiet.

"I'm taking Quilla to Puerto Rico for the week."

The line stays quiet.

"Whaddup, Usher?"

"Yo, man, you trippin' for sure. How you gone leave town when somebody tryna fuck with us? Damn, nigga, we need to be retaliatin' and lettin' these fools know we run this shit and to *respect* that."

I put the phone between my ear and shoulder as I bend down to pick up my son and the bottle sitting next to him. "So everybody and they momma know we got hit. I can tell you heard some shit—*in the street*—about who did it. So we retaliate and that's more news hot as hell—*in the street*—and before you know it we got the po-po deep in our asses for murder *and* drug charges. Now all of that shit behind twenty-five grand. Hell no, man. Come on. Don't fall into the trap, kid."

"So we just let this shit ride and look like punks and fuckin' busters and shit to everybody?"

"No, we chill and let things cool off. So I'm headed to Puerto Rico and you might as well grab a bitch and head somewhere too and just chill, man. Fuck it. The grind grindin' on me."

"Man, I don't think you should go to fuckin' Puerto Rico."

I start to feed my son his bottle but Usher has me tense as a bitch and I didn't want Dashon to feel that vibe, so I set him back down. I feel pressure.

Pressure to not live my own fucking life the way I want to.

Pressure to be some fake-ass gangster.

Pressure to stay in the fucking game.

Pressure to be other motherfuckers' meal ticket.

All that pressure had my neck tight as shit.

Fuck that.

"I'll be back next week and nobody gone make a move until I get back. Unless it's an emergency I'm not even takin' no calls."

"Yo . . . I understand. I don't agree but . . . yo, have a good time, ya heard me?"

"Peace."

I toss the phone onto the bed and notice Quilla standing in the doorway. She's only dressed in a towel. I flex my shoulders and bend down to pick up my son. "Hurry up and get dressed, Quilla."

"I thought you wanted to talk?" she says.

I smile when Dashon sucks away at the nipple on the

bottle like he tryna hurt something. "Naw, I changed my mind."

"About getting out or talking about getting out."

I just shrug.

She stands there for a minute but I stay focused on my son. Soon I hear the bathroom door close behind her. I have a lot of decisions to make, but one thing I know for sure is that my son is the best damn thing that ever happened to me. I love him and now I feel how my parents wanted more for my ass growing up because I want more for him. I want him safe. I want him happy.

I want him to be proud of me.

18

The Playa

Guess who's back?

Damn right. Me. Life is back just the way I want it. True, I have to fuck a dinosaur damn near every night but other than that I'm back on point. Polette didn't even ask for money for bills. Her SSI check covers everything. All she wants from me is a stiff one—be it a drink or my dick. Thank God that if I got her the drink—or drinks—early enough, then her ugly ass would pass out before I had to lay pipe.

Once I bought the bitch an economy pack of douche and lied, telling her I only love to fuck doggy-style—with her face down in a pillow. Shee-it, the pussy wadn't half bad.

I roll over in bed and pick up my prepaid cell phone to check the time. 11:30 a.m. I stretch out all the kinks from sleepin' in a fuckin' double. "Polette," I call out, sittin' up in bed.

The bedroom door opens and she sticks her head in, a blunt already blazing from her wet-ass mouth. I snap my fingers and hold out my hand. She strolls her ass right on over and plucks the blunt out her mouth to give to me. I ignore the funky smell of her spit on the tip as I hit it.

Polette drops her robe and climbs into bed—so that's my clue to roll out. "It just said on the news that Tweedle Dumb and Tweedle Dumber took a plea for six months for rollin' around with that dead body."

I just shake my head. It was all over the news when them fools, Pop-Pop and Rollo, got caught trying to cash the check of that dead man. Crazy shit happens in the hood all the time, but that shit got to be about the craziest shit ever. "Them drunks probably happy as fuck for them three hots and a cot," I tell her as I lay out my new black-and-gold Omavi fitted tee and jeans on the bed.

Polette laughs, showing off her raggedy-ass grill. "Yeah, three hots and a cot but no shots. They ass in that bitch feignin'. Trust."

I pick up my new gold-and-black Kashi Kicks as I cut my eyes over at her. Since her ass could fuck up a twelve-pack of King Cobras by her damn self, she ought to fucking know. I ignored her spreading her bony legs to play in her own gray-haired pussy. My mind and my dick is on other things. Better things. Like my new bitch Trina waiting for me at the Knights Inn for a fuckfest to top all fuckfests. She married to this cop, so we sneakin'.

That's the best fuck in the world. And trust me, givin' it hard to the wife of some fool in blue make the pussy even better.

"Where you goin', baby?"

I start to ignore her ass but since I need to borrow her beat-up Crown Vic and get some gas money, I decided to play it cool. "I'm going to pick up a new shipment of bags to sell," I lie to her ass over my shoulder as I leave the bedroom and walk down the hall to the bathroom.

I wish the motor in Shaterica's car hadn't broke down or I would be still cruisin' in *that* motherfucker. Ever since I moved in with Polette I only went back in Shaterica's apartment to have a private spot to get my dick blown by Delia. Well, I used to until they evicted Shaterica for nonpayment. I know by now she got to be in that bitch wonderin' what the fuck goin' on, since we ain't spoke in a minute—but what she expect? Shit, that bitch doin' ten years. Fuck the dumb shit.

Nosy motherfuckers 'round here talkin' mad shit 'cause I moved in with Polette, but fuck that, a nigga got to live and until I find me a better set I ain't leavin' Bentley Manor or Polette.

In the bathroom that is way too pink, I use a wet rag to wipe away some of the splattered toothpaste on the mirror. I lean forward to check out my face. My perfect face. I got my whole fine-ass life ahead of me. Did her dumb ass really think I was gonna sit around here waitin' for her for ten years? I'm supposed to deny all these bitches out here a chance to get at me for ten years? Shit, I'll be in my thirties by then. Fuck *that* dumb shit.

Man, forget Shaterica's big whop-up ass. She made a choice to cop to the murder and life is about choices. There is no way in hell she coulda convince my ass to do the same thing. A playa like me? I'm too together for that shit for real. Only advice I got for her now is don't drop the soap. I laugh in the mirror as I walk out.

After a quick shower, I spray on some imitation Polo cologne and walk out to the bedroom. I am so ready to get to the motel 'cause that trick got a way of sucking my dick that makes me cum so hard that I think she pulling the cord out that motherfucker. Plus, her ass got a little bit of change and a nigga like me need a new pair of kicks.

"Momma, I need new sneakers."

I go still as hell and look at myself hard in the mirror. That voice of a child sounded clear as hell around me. Clear and familiar.

I tried to shake that shit off as I put toothpaste on my brush. Fuck memory lane around this motherfucker. Fuck it.

"You want new sneakers. I got your yella ass some sneakers. . . ."

I can't help my mouth from curling up like I smell sour shit. It's all about hate.

"You better use what your yella ass got to get what the fuck you want."

I hate her. I hate all bitches. . . .

Life was fucked up for me and my momma from jump street. Ever since I could remember, we lived in shit filled up with so many rats and roaches that I felt like we was coppin' a squat in they shit. Sometimes we stayed in those little-ass studio apartments but never nothin' bigger than a one bedroom.

Never.

I looked out the cracked window of our latest shit hole and watched the drunks stumblin' in and out of the liquor store across the street. I stared and stared until I saw my momma walk out and I don't know if I'm happy or not that she headed home.

She a messy drunk. Not messy in the way she looks, because my momma was beautiful with her long and thick jet-black hair that made her fair complexion seem even brighter, especially when she wore that bright red lipstick of hers. Men was always whistlin' and carryin' on when she walked by. Always tellin' her how pretty she was. Or beggin' her to let them pay her bills.

She was still young—just twelve years older than me, making her twenty. Sometimes I wonder why she drink like that. Why she so scared to not be drunk? Is that the only thing that stops her from cryin' so much at night when she thought my little young ass was sleepin'? What makes her so mad at me?

I focused my eyes on Momma stumblin' her drunk ass across the street in her tight jeans, tank top, and heels. Her long hair is blowing in the wind as she tries her best to walk like she ain't already drunk.

Soon I hear her makin' her way up the rickety stairs. I can almost count when she stumbles over that eighth stair that is loose. "Shit," she swears, her voice echoin' in the beat-down and battered hallway.

I was just eight and for me my momma was the only person I could rely on—sometimes that was scary as shit. When she was sober she was always mad and when she was drunk . . .

The front door burst open and Momma stumbles in side-ways on her stilettos. Momma always wore stilettos. I don't think I ever remembered her drunk ass in sneakers or flats.

"Get your red ass out that window," she tells me while she sit her bag on the scratched metal dinette set with only one chair and walks over to the sink. I guess that's the way she say hello to me after leavin' me alone all day and most of the night in a hot-ass apartment.

"Momma, I'm hungry."

She stopped pourin' that gin she loved into my old Atlanta Falcons mug to look down at me. "Why your ass wait good 'til I get home to fuckin' chill to talk 'bout your ass hungry? Damn, you know how to blow my fuckin' high. Shit."

My stomach growled and a pain hit my ass that felt like

a knife to my gut. I put my hand to it like it would help it
from hurtin'.

My momma just sucked her teeth and stumbled over to
slump down onto the bright-red sofa that looked like a big
pair of lips. I settled down on the floor in front of our little
thirteen-inch black-and-white TV. Really, my little ass was
cryin' and I didn't want her to see it. I was not going to let
her see me cry.

It was okay for her to sit up all night cryin' into her bottles
but when I shed a tear that meant an ass-whippin' for me.

"Sick of this shit," she slurs. "How 'bout me, motherfucker?
How 'bout what I want? Shit."

My stomach drops and I close my eyes and wish I could be
anywhere but there. I was just waitin' to feel her hand upside
my head or her foot across my ass. Momma liked to take all
her drama out on me when she drunk and I got plenty of old
bruises to prove it. Plenty of 'em.

"Gimme, gimme, fuckin' gimme."

Her voice gets louder and louder. A gold shoe goes flyin'
past my head. My heart beats like crazy and I wish like hell
I had somewhere to hide. The door to the bathroom was already hangin' like a loose tooth. I tried to hide in there one
time and she kicked that thin wooden bitch open like she was
the Hulk or some shit.

"You know what. Fuck that. I'M SICK OF THIS SHIT.
I'M . . . SICK . . . OF . . . THIS . . . SHIT!"

I ducked because I knew the feel of her hands, her fists,
and her feet wadn't far off. WHAP! To the back my head.

THUD! *One to my lower back. Pain darted all across my body as she hit and kick me time and time and time again.*

"Momma, I need this," *she screamed as she bent down over me, the smell of gin so strong on my face.* "Momma, I need that."

Two punches to my face for somethin' I asked for in the past. And I only asked for things I needed. I never asked for things I wanted, like games, candy, or some shit. Just the necessary shit: food, shoes without holes, pants that wasn't highwaters.

I just closed my eyes and prayed for her to get tired of beatin' on me. "Look at me! Look at me!" *she screamed, grabbin' my face and turnin' my head toward her so hard that I thought my neck was gonna snap.*

"I'm sick of you. You look just like you no-good, red-ass daddy."

Spit from her mouth sprayed against my face. "Momma—"

"Momma this and Momma fuckin' that. Call your no-good daddy and ask for shit!"

She let my face go long enough to slap the shit out of me. Whap! *Tears filled my eyes and my face stung like hell.*

"Don't ask me for shit. Get your little ass out there and hustle like I do. Give me a fuckin' break, motherfucker."

THUD! THUD!

Two punches to my jaw.

I thanked God when she gave me one last hard nudge with her shoe before she stumbled back over to fall back into those lips of the couch. I laid there, fightin' like hell not to cry, and promisin' myself I was gonna do what I gotta do to take care of myself from now on. . . .

When I was twelve and our thirty-year-old neighbor Ms. Hand pulled me into her apartment and offered me a dollar to eat her pussy, I learned my value. Women wanted to be with me and they were willin' to pay for it.

I didn't have no fuckin' choice.

My looks and my dick made it possible for me to run away from them ass whippin's and my crazy drunk of a mother.

I hated the tears that filled my eyes. I hated them almost as much as I hated my mother. She taught me early that women ain't shit.

They don't deserve love. Trust. Fidelity. Honesty.

None of that shit.

I ain't got nothing for them bitches but what my bitch of a mother had for me. Nothin' but a hard fuckin' way to go.

Fuck it.

19

The Pimp

I'm tryin'. I'm really fuckin' tryin', but this shit is workin' my nerves. After reachin' out and doin' that whole father-daughter crap, all I get for my troubles are a bunch of eye rolls. So far private schools haven't yielded much results. The last time I got called into a school it was because Corrine and some other badass teenager decided to experiment on each other in the girls' bathroom.

My daughter, a lesbian?

Hell, why not, especially when you considered the circus crew she calls a family.

"Why do you care what I do?" she challenged me yesterday as we rode home.

"I really don't fuckin' know," I answered honestly, irritated that all my efforts were being wasted.

"What—you want to kick me out the house now?"

I turned to her with my face scrunched up. "Why do

you keep asking me that? If I wanted you gone, believe me, your ass would've been ghosted by now," I told her for the hundredth time. And just like before, she had a look in her eye that said she didn't believe me.

I'm out of my element on how to deal with her.

It's late when Anderson and I roll up to Club Diamond. The spot is jumpin', pussies are poppin', and money is definitely flowin'. But I get a nice surprise when Fat Joe tells me I have a visitor waitin' for me in my office.

I renamed Tracy Jenkins Chocolate Angel the moment she walked into my first strip club. Her skin literally is the color of rich, dark chocolate, but her creamy center is nothing but pure strawberry. She performed in a coupla my first Red Light District movies. She was doing double anal back when the shit was considered taboo.

Renee never liked her.

Destiny liked her even less.

I was whipped. At least for a little while until she just up and quit the business. I was surprised when she left—stunned when she didn't return. Well, up until she dropped off the kid.

"Hey, Sweet," Tracy greets me the moment I enter my office at Club Diamond.

I'm impressed the body is still bangin' and her voice still has that hypnotic husk to it. No shit. If she tested clean, I could get an easy five grand an hour off her ass.

"Please tell me you came for a job interview," I say, making my way over to the bar.

"No. Actually, I came here to talk to you about Corrine." She draws a deep breath. "I want her back."

I try, but I can't ignore the sudden tightening in my chest. "What you think, I'm runnin' some elaborate babysitting service?" I ask. "You drop her off and pick her up whenever the fuck you please? Is that it?"

"No. It's not like that."

I pour a small brandy. "Then what is it like?"

She draws in a deep breath; takes her time to weigh her words. "I was just having a bit of financial trouble. That's all. Everything is fine now."

"Is that right?"

She braids her hands before her and twitches nervously. "I just want Corrine to come back home."

"She is home—her new home."

A lopsided smile hook a corner of her lips. "C'mon, now. Corrine is my daughter."

"Then you should have kept her."

Tracy's eyes narrow. "Stop playing. What the hell do you want with a fifteen-year-old girl?"

I shrug. "I don't know. Maybe I'd like to finish raising her."

She laughs in my face. "What—you want her turnin' tricks for you? Shit. I thought you had more class than to put a fifteen-year-old on payroll. Let alone your own daughter. But wait. Didn't you used to pimp out your own momma?"

I slam my glass back onto the glass bar. "Don't fuck with me."

Tracy closes her big damn mouth, but continues to glare.

"Corrine is pretty fucked up," I tell her. "The girl has been kicked out of three different schools in three weeks. Stripping for boys, experimenting with girls, and gettin' high. What the hell have you been teaching her?"

"Why the hell do you care?"

"She's fifteen!" The office falls silent as I try to get my shit back together. "Look. I did what I had to do when I was her age because I didn't have a choice. It was either slingin' pussy or slingin' dope. Corrine doesn't have to go down that road. She could be the first in my fucked-up family to get out this bullshit game. I have enough money to send her to the best schools, treat her to finer things."

"She'd still be nothing but a pimp and a ho's daughter," Tracy counters. "Some things are just in the blood. You should know that better than anybody."

I shake my head, certain that if I'd been involved earlier things would've been different for Corrine. "You should've told me about her sooner. She should've had a better chance. That's all I'm saying."

Tracy looks at me as if we've never met. "Don't tell me that Sweet Diamondtrim Tavon Johnson actually gives a fuck about somebody other than himself."

I toss back my double shot of brandy and enjoy the burn as it went down.

"Save that pimp with the golden-heart routine for someone else. How the hell are you going to pretend that you never knew about Corrine? Your wife made it clear that you didn't want any part of our child sixteen years ago."

"What the fuck are you talking about? Renee didn't know about Corrine."

"Ha!" Tracy rolls her eyes. "Of course she knew. I told her my damn self."

My head starts to spin and it doesn't have a damn thing to do with the brandy. "I don't fuckin' believe you."

"Believe what the fuck you want. Her ass has always been able to pull the wool over your eyes. You probably never missed the money she's been paying me to stay lost all these years."

The blood in my veins turns cold. "What the fuck did you say about my money?"

Finally the other corner of her lips curl upward. "Paid me a cool hundred G's when I was three months pregnant to get rid of the baby."

"But—"

"I kept the baby anyway. Then when Corrine was born and I came to your place to introduce you to your daughter, Renee started paying me monthly to stay away."

"How much?"

"Fifteen thousand a month."

I quickly do the math. "That fuckin' bitch."

"Yeah, well. Then she stopped payin'."

"So you dropped the kid off at my momma's."

"It got her attention."

The things I did to Sabrina have nothing on what I

want to do to my own wife right now. "What are you doing back?" I ask, though I suspect the answer.

Tracy reaches inside her purse and withdraws a check. "I got another hundred Gs. I swear, poppin' out Corrine has been like hittin' the lottery."

I slowly walk over to her, my eyes locked onto the check.

Tracy quickly tucks it back into her purse, but she never saw my backhand until it was too late. Her head snaps back and a dark burgundy imprint is stamped against the right side of her face while blood trickles from her bottom lip.

"I tell you what," I say, somehow managing to sound calm. "You can either keep that check and walk out of here or you can give it back and take Corrine." I meet her eyes. Where she was once paid to keep Corrine from me, I'm now offering to pay to keep her.

Tracy lifts her chin. "And my monthly payment?"

I swear it's all I can do not to beat this bitch to the ground. "Your monthly payment will continue. *I'll* be writing the check."

Her smile returns. "Yep. Just like the muthafuckin' lottery."

Once Tracy leaves my office, Anderson drives me home like he tryna qualify for the Indy 500. I tear through the house looking for Renee's sorry ass.

Nobody is home—including Corrine—who continues to ignore curfew on the regular.

"These damn bitches are going to be the death of me, I swear." I blow up Renee's cell phone and then pace the floor waiting for her to call me back. After half an hour, I start checking all the clubs and studios. When that didn't work, I called her friends, family, and a couple of lovers she has on the side that she doesn't think I know about. That bitch has to be somewhere.

It's damn near midnight when Renee strolls her ass up in here like everything is everything and she didn't have a care in the world. I jump her ass like a Saturday-night raider on Land Rover.

"Where the fuck you been?"

"Out, nigga. What?" She snaps back. "You tryna lock a bitch down or somethin'?"

I give her a good backhand and loved the feeling of it so much that I gave her another one. When she manages to center her head again, her angry glare matches my own.

"You got some muthafuckin' explaining to do."

"The bitch talked, didn't she?"

"You damn right she did." I start pacing. "How the fuck could you do something like this?"

Renee lifts her chin defiantly. "What, you want to beat my ass now?"

"Believe me. I'm thinking about it."

She rolls her eyes. "What the fuck ever. I did what I had to do to keep mine."

"What the fuck are you talkin' about?"

Renee pushes past me. "Don't act like you don't know."

"Bitch, don't you walk away from me. I will stomp your ass into the ground for this foul shit. Trust. I ain't in the mood for your nonsense. Not tonight."

She turns around. "What? You think it's easy being married to you? I let you put me through too many fuckin' changes to let some two-bit stripper steal you away from me. You think I was just going to watch you go play house with some other bitch cuz she can give you kids and I can't? It's bad enough that I have to share you with that he-she freak Destin. At least I know his ass can't turn up pregnant and he keeps his shit clean."

"So that's why you asked for me to get snipped. I'd already fathered a kid." I shake my head. "You're fuckin' crazy."

"*I'm* fuckin' crazy?" she screams. "The minute you found out about Corrine you were all set to play Daddy. You think you'd been any different sixteen years ago? You would've left me. And you know it." She drew in a deep breath. "I remember how you were with your *Chocolate Angel.* You rarely brought your ass home.

"Do you know what it's like wondering every day which one of these young tricks is gonna steal you away? Every day they turn eighteen while I get older. I've been turnin' tricks, suckin' dicks, and makin' movies for half my damn life. All just to make you happy. I'm number one in this bitch and that's how it's gonna stay!"

Renee stares at me with tears running down her face while I stand here feeling like an asshole. "I'm not going to let you lay this shit on me. You've always had a choice. You knew what and who I was from the jump. If you're so unhappy—"

"What—I can leave? Is that what you're going to say?" She draws another deep breath as more tears fall from her eyes. "That's just it, Tavon. Every day, I try to leave you. Every. Fuckin'. Day. And I just can't."

"Then maybe *I* should leave," I tell her. I grab my jacket from off the back of the chair and head toward the front door.

"Tavon, where are you going?"

I don't answer.

"Tavon!"

I slam the door.

"TAVON!"

Since I hadn't bothered calling Anderson, I select the Porsche from the garage and hit the open highway. I desperately need to put some distance between me and this sorry-ass situation. The hard part is I've always been up front with Renee.

I don't want to own Renee's pain. I have my own to deal with and right now I have a pretty messed-up fifteen-year-old and apparently that shit is my fault, too.

I make my way out to Buckhead. This time to the lake house that Destiny uses as her own crib. Whenever things get fucked up between me and Renee, Destiny always has a way of cooling me down, relieving my stress. If I remember correctly this was her night off, so maybe she's home. I think about calling, but fuck it. Even if she's not there, I can still chill out and clear my mind.

I slip my key into the lock and enter. I'm surprised to hear the smooth sounds of Teddy Pendergrass playing throughout the place. Teddy P meant Destiny had company. Maybe they wouldn't mind a third party.

I close the door and ease out of my jacket as I make my way to the bar in the living room. I definitely need another drink. Just then I hear the soft sounds of a feminine moan drift from the bedroom. It's a woman tonight.

"Oh shit. Oh shit," the breathless female says.

I toss back my drink and begin to peel out of my shirt. Destiny and I have shared plenty of women over the years. Can't see why tonight would be any different.

I smile as my buzz kicks in.

"Fuck me, motherfucker. Fuck me," the now familiar voice barks above the bucking bed. It sounds like he has a wild one on his hands.

I frown and head toward the bedroom with a smile on my face. When I open the door, my heart stops.

I blink once, sure that my eyes are playing tricks on me and it's not my fifteen-year-old daughter straddling my best friend *and* lover.

"Oh shit!" Corrine jumps up and scrambles off the bed.

"What the FUCK?!" I roar.

"Wait, Tavon. It's not what you think!" Destiny says.

I charge forward as Destiny's hands fly up in surrender. "Let me explain."

That's all he got out of his muthafuckin' mouth before I slam my fist against his jaw. I hear Corrine racing out of the room, sobbing, but I don't give a fuck. All my attention is focused on killing this motherfucker right here. I throw punches so hard, it feels like I'm hitting cement blocks.

"You have lost your muthafuckin' mind!" I shout. "*You-sick-fuck!* I'm gonna kill you."

"Sweet, no!" Corrine jumps on my back and tries to stop my swinging, but she's nothing more than a gnat.

"Please, stop!" Corrine shouts.

I hear Destiny's bones cracking beneath my fist.

"Stop! You're gonna kill him."

Shit. That's the motherfuckin' point.

"Please! Stop! Please!"

I don't know how, but Corrine manages to reach through my rage. I step away from the bed, Corrine still on my back and Destiny a crumpled, bloody heap. Somehow his ass is still breathing.

"You stay the fuck away from me and my family," I growl at him. When he doesn't answer, I charge the bed again. "Do you fuckin' hear me, motherfucker?"

"Y-yes," he croaks over a blood bubble, his hands still trying to show his surrender.

"I swear if I ever see your ass again, you're a dead motherfucker!"

Corrine pulls me toward the bedroom door. "You hear me, motherfucker? You stay the fuck away!"

20

The Killer

"Hey, nigga. I hear you need a job."

I glance over my shoulder and light up when I see a blast from the past. "M. Dawg!" I hold my fist up for a coupla dabs and a shoulder bump. "Ah, man. What the fuck are you doin' here?" I glance around the Circle K gas station to see if he hangin' with anyone else I know.

A broad smile frames M. Dawg's face. He's still a short motherfucker, but his waistline has definitely exploded over the years. "Just chillin'. Came up here for some papers. You know how I roll."

"That's seven dollars and fifty-four cents," the foreign dude behind the register says as if bored waiting for me to pay for my shit.

"Here. Let me get that shit for you," M. Dawg says, pulling out a wad of money from his hip pocket.

"Nah. Nah. That's not necessary," I insist, pulling out a few crumpled-up dollar bills.

M. Dawg just laughs. "Nigga, please. Let me do this. I ain't seen your ass in a hot minute. I got this shit."

It's not easy stuffin' my pride back into my chest, but somehow I manage and grab the small plastic sack from the counter with a tight, "Thanks, man. I owe you one."

"Shit, nigga. You don't owe me nothin'. After all the shit we've been through?" He pays for his rollin' papers and two forties.

I bounce my head up and down but I can't help but feel M. Dawg's presence here isn't a wild coincidence.

"So how you and your girl doin'?" he asks, and we turn to head out of the gas station.

"We doin' good," I lie. "You know how we do."

He nods as if he knows what I'm saying is bullshit. Zoey lost her job last week and money is beyond tight. Some money was missing out of the petty cash box and when word got around that she was shacked up with an ex-con, those white bitches wasted no time in letting Zoey's ass go.

"So are you lookin' for a job?" he asks.

"I'm only lookin' for legit work. You know, shit that comes with a W-2," I tell him. "I ain't looking to get caught up again."

M. Dawg starts laughin'. "Oh. You a proud nigga now, huh? You can't eat pride."

I keep smilin' as I start to head up Holloway Parkway.

M. Dawg stops by this fly-as-shit, candy-apple-red Hummer. "Wanna lift?"

I pause long enough to catch my breath, but shake my head at his tempting offer.

"C'mon, nigga. Get in the car. We got a lot of catchin' up to do."

"Zoey is waitin' for me," I say.

He doesn't buy my shit at all. "Nigga, stop trippin' and get in the car."

I hesitate one last time and then finally give in. The minute I open the door, my ass is trippin'. No shit, this had to be the tightest shit I've ever planted my ass in. "This is all you?"

"You know it." He slams the car door behind him and starts it up. The engine is smooth like honey, the interior seats are more comfortable than the sofa set in Zoey's crib. Damn, everybody livin' large these days—everyone but me.

It doesn't surprise me when M. Dawg pulls out into Holloway Parkway and rolls past Bentley Manor.

"I meant that shit about a job, man. We go way back and I'm more than willing to help a brotha out."

"Thanks, man but—"

"Hey. Hear me out. I'm talkin' about a coupla Gs a week. Shit that's gonna get you straight at yo crib and getcha baby momma off yo back."

I drop the smile. "Who says I'm havin' trouble with—"

"Nigga, save it," he says, still smiling like Lucifer himself. "We boys. No need for all this needless bullshit. I've heard about yo situation. Ain't no reason for Zoey to be on my phone cryin' and shit."

"Zoey called you?"

"Look. Don't be mad at her," he snaps; his gaze turns hard. "Z is a good woman. I've done my fair share of checkin' in on her while you were locked down. Hell, I consider her family. Frankly, I'm a little insulted that you ain't been man enough to holla at your boy."

What the fuck?! I twist in my seat as anger boils in my veins. I can't believe the shit I'm hearing. "Nigga, don't tell me you fuckin' with what's mine."

M. Dawg pulls his shit over to the side of the road, parks, and turns toward me. "I called myself doin' yo ass a favor," he says evenly. "Is this how you gonna thank me? Hell, if it wasn't for me, her ass would've been on the street a few years ago. Maybe you prefer her walkin' the street or slidin' down one of Sweet's poles over at Club Diamond. Is that it?"

"Don't test me, Dawg. Did you forget who the fuck you're talkin' to?"

"Nah. Fuck that. I did yo ass a favor. I paid for her school and loaned her the down payment for that piece of shit she's drivin'—all because I thought we were boys."

A killer calm comes over me. "Did you fuck with my girl?" I ask him.

M. Dawg boldly meets my stare. "Better me than some nigga you don't know, right?"

"Fuck you, nigga!" I reach for one of the forties and bust that shit over his head. M. Dawg instantly slumped over to the side. I didn't give a shit and continued to slice this motherfucker until he was good and dead.

I'm a fuckin' tornado when I make it back to Bentley Manor. Gettin' rid of M. Dawg's body and then hittin' up an old chop shop outfit to take care of that big-ass Hummer was like ridin' an old bike.

Once you learn this shit, you never forget.

I storm into Zoey's apartment and when I slam the door behind me, she jumps ten feet off the couch.

"Where the fuck have you been?"

I glance out the venetian blinds, check the street. There's just the regular crackheads and foot soldiers patrolling the area.

"Is that blood on your shirt?" Zoey asks.

I finally turn my attention to her, my blood still cold as ice. "What the fuck you been doing with M. Dawg and shit while I was gone?" I launch toward her.

Her eyes widen as she springs off the sofa. She tries running toward the bedroom, but I grab a fistful of her hair and snatch her ass back. "Where the fuck you think you goin'?" I turn and body-slam her ass straight into the wall.

"Demarcus, please!"

"Save that shit, bitch." I take her head and ram it again. Her eyes look dazed. "You had another nigga runnin' up in my shit? My own boys! What the fuck is wrong with you?"

"I'm so-rry," she sobs, still tryna get away.

"You sorry? I don't give a fuck about you bein' sorry. How you gonna violate me like that, huh? How you callin' motherfuckers cryin' and shit and telling them what the fuck goes on in this motherfucker? Am I your man or what?" My hands wrap around her neck and I begin to squeeze.

"I-I . . ."

"What, bitch? I can't hear you." Her face is turning purple. "Your ass musta thought I've gone soft. Is that it?"

She struggles to shake her head, but she manages to catch a few sips of air.

"I had to put a nigga to sleep because of your hookin' ass. You selling my shit?"

"N-no."

"Yeah, you were. Don't fuckin' lie to me. Nigga just had me up in his ride tellin' me whatcha been doin'. I oughta kill your ass right now. That's what you want me to do, ain't it?" She slumps to the floor, but I kneel down over her. My hands still squeezin'.

"N-no. P-please. I-I'm so-rry," she gasps.

It would be so easy just to end this shit. Snap her neck in half. Put us both out of our misery. She reaches up, her hands soft against my face.

"P-please, baby. D-don't." Her eyes roll.

I love her. I hate her. I can't live without her.

That's the kind of stench you can't wash off.

Quite suddenly, I release her and fall over onto the floor beside her. I hear her wheeze in a breath.

And then another.

And another. She starts choking on air while I close my eyes and shame washes over me and tears leak from the corners of my eyes. What the fuck did I do? How did I veer so far off track?

Zoey rolls toward me, her heart-wrenching sobs tear at my heart. "I-I'm so so-rry, baby," she croaks, pressing her full lips against my face. "I'm so sorry." Her wet face brushes against mine as I wrap my arms around her.

"It's okay, baby. We'll get through this. We always do."

21

The Playa

Black people know they can do the dumbest shit sometimes.

I'm standing on Holloway Parkway down by the Circle K tryna sell these damn Pucci, Fuey Vuitoon, and Poach bags. That's hard as hell to do when the first of the month gone already. These birds ain't good for shit after the tenth. Just one fuckin' bag sold all day. *Humph.* Just a bunch of bullshit.

I reach in the pocket of my jeans for a smoke and squint my eyes while I look over at some chick and five heads of children climbin' out of a car down the street. I frown like "what the fuck" when the teenage boy walks back to the trunk to pull out those fake-ass flowers you find on cemetery plots and shit.

As I look around I see everybody out this motherfucker lookin' at they ass while they puttin' all that flower and shit by a tree.

"Damn, Lex good as hell to bring her kids after that shit Junior did to her."

I turn my head and see two young birds strainin' they head to look down the street too. "Yo, I got them designer bags straight from New York," I tell them, holdin' out my arms to show them the bags I'm holdin' like I'm Lenny from *Good Times.*

"Naw, we good," the high yella one with the freckles say.

I just shrug and ignore they broke asses while I peep the scene about half a block down the street. I heard about all that shit that went down last summer up in the Manor. Shit, who hadn't heard about it. Two dead bodies. Some bitch trickin' on the low gettin' slashed in the face. Findin' out my homeboy Junior was livin' life foul as hell on the down low. Shit, Junior was straight wildin' out fuckin' dudes and chicks. Oh, I knew that nigga but I ain't know his ass *like that.* Matter of fact, I try to not to think about that crazy shit and here's these motherfuckers layin' out flowers and shit where that white bitch shot his ass dead. Must be the anniversary or some shit.

Who would want to remember that? Man, black people know they got some shit with they ass sometimes.

I take another drag off my cigarette and squint my eyes as a silver Honda pulls up behind it. This fine-ass bitch with braids down her back and nails long enough to make you wonder how she wash her ass gets out to walk up to them. I ain't gone lie. The sight of her ass in them tight jeans make me wanna fuck.

"There go WooWoo lesbo ass," one of them birds say with plenty of attitude.

Lesbo? That makes me look at that ass long and hard, 'cause I want it even more.

"I can't believe that bitch still goin' to visit Has after that he/she killed her fuckin' husband," the other bird puts in.

I'm eavesdroppin' like a motherfucker. I missed that little bit of news floatin' around Bentley Manor.

"Fuck a dildo. I need that live dick that pumps and gets warm when I make that bitch cum, ya heard me."

"I don't know. That fake-ass dick Has threw at that bitch that day was big as hell. I ain't run cross no real dick to top *that* shit."

Them birds laugh and I hear them slap hands.

I let out a circle of smoke and watch while Lexi and WooWoo and all them damn kids climb back into their cars and pull the fuck off. Now that's some drama for your ass.

I check my cell phone. I been out here damn near all day and I ain't sold but one bag? Man, I need to get the fuck from 'round this bitch. Ready to get out the heat, I snatch up my bags and head back to the Manor.

Man, I'm sick of fuckin' strugglin'. It's time for a fine nigga like me to do a Beyoncé and upgrade up out of Bentley Manor, Bankhead, and the hood, period. If I fuck around and get the right set in L.A. or New York a nigga like me ain't workin' no fuckin' more. I didn't get away with murder to be strugglin' like a bitch.

As soon as I walk through the gates of Bentley Manor I see Delia sittin' on somebody's Caddy smokin' a cigarette. She looks over at me and looks away. For the first time in a long damn time her ass don't look like she high or feenin' to get high. She still dressed bummy as hell in a faded black wifebeater and jeans that's too big for her skinny ass.

I see Miz Cleo and Miz Osceola got they eye on me as I walk over to Delia. I don't bother to wave to they nosy ass. Them old bitches don't do shit but smack they bats in their hands whenever they see me. They better be glad I don't go for silver pussy 'cause they ass need a good ass-whippin' or a good dickin' down.

"Whaddup, Delia," I ask her, sitting my box of bags on the ground while I lean back against the car next to her.

"Leave me alone, Rhak, I got shit on my mind," she tells me, her hand shakin' and shit as she lift the cigarette to her mouth.

My eyes drop down to watch the way her lips press down on the tip. My dick comes to life. "I know how to get shit off your mind," I tell her, tryin' my damndest to give her the look. Not that a head like Delia had to be seduced and shit. All I need is two fuckin' dollars. Eight quarters. Ten dimes. Forty nickels.

"I'm sick of livin' like this," she admits in this voice that is just a little bit louder than a damn whisper. When she do turn and look at me, there are tears in her eyes. Tears and torture.

Why the fuck she droppin' all this heavy shit on me?

"Then carry your ass to rehab." Attitude is in my voice. I ain't got time for no fuckin' sob stories.

She just kinda laughs and takes another long pull off her cigarette. "Too much fuckin' memories I can't run from. Too much withdrawals. Too much fuckin' work. Shit, it's easier to just get high." She laughs again but I can tell she don't think shit funny.

"You think I don't know I fell off? I don't know how I look? My grill fucked up. My body whack. My life ain't shit. My family won't fuck with me. I ain't seen my kids in months. You think I wanna be a fuckin' crackhead 'round here suckin' stick sweaty-ass dicks and balls to get high? You think I wanna feel like less than a woman? You think I wanna be livin' in an apartment with five other heads and shit?" Her voice shaky as hell as she sucks back the fuckin' tears from fallin'. In the hood sometimes there ain't no time for cryin'. Not when it's all about survivin'.

I think of my momma and her own demons. I remember the way she used to cry before, during, and after she got drunk. "How you get on that shit?" I ask her.

Delia gets real silent as she looks off at some shit I can't see. "People judge motherfuckers on drugs. Say we weak.

We stupid. We ain't shit. It's a lot of motherfuckers running from they life. Running from they memories. Running from shit they can't change. Not everybody handle shit the same way, you know. It's hard gettin' off this shit. I want to get high so bad right now. My body callin' for it. Fuckin' with me. You know?"

Okay, now this bitch depressin' the fuck out of me.

"Sometimes I lay there and I want it so bad and I don't want it at the same time. Back and forth. Fightin', tryna leave that shit alone. It fucks with me so bad that sometimes I just wanna die." She holds up her hands and wipes away the tears that fall like she tryna erase them motherfuckers.

"I can't remember the last time I fucked some dude just because I wanted to."

Okay, fuckin'. Now we back on familiar territory and she ain't touchin' on shit inside of me that hit too close to home about my momma. Too close to home about Shaterica. Too close to home about all the other bitches I done run through. Fuck 'em.

"Where Polette?" she asks me.

I squint my eyes against the sun as a car drives by slow as hell, vibratin' from the bass of his sound system. "Her and her sister went to visit they mother—"

"Fuck me."

The rest of the words die down from my mouth. I look at her and I can see she serious and sober as hell. *Humph.* This bitch was just singing a sad song 'bout she tired of trickin' and smokin' dope. What the fuck ever. "I ain't got no money," I lie, even as I slide my hand inside my pocket and finger the forty dollars I made from sellin' that powder blue Poach bag.

She drops the cigarette to the asphalt and then mashes it flat with the tip of her sandals. "I didn't ask you for none."

A free fuck? Shee-it. If her pussy is anywhere near as good as her head, then fuck the dumb shit. She wanna feel like a woman, then she got the right motherfucker for that job.

"I'm going up to the apartment. Wait ten minutes and come up behind me." I bend down, grab my box, and stroll my ass across the lot into the buildin'. Even as I walk into the apartment I am countin' in my head how many condoms I got. Listen, I love pussy but I ain't tryna die for it. Findin' out that Junior ran though the women in this motherfucker like it was his personal pussy playland got me nervous as a bitch, since his wife made it clear that his ass gave her AIDS.

Fuck that. Better safe than fuckin' sorry.

"Yes . . . yes . . . yes!"

That all that Delia's keep sayin' over and over and over again as I work my hips to send my dick in and out of her pussy. Sometimes she says it all soft and low like a whisper. Sometimes she bitin' her bottom lip and then screamin' that shit to the rooftops. But that's all she keep sayin'. Yes. Yes. Yes.

She spreads her legs wider in the center of Polette's bed and I stop fuckin' her to bend my head and look down into her face while my dick throb against her walls. Her tight and warm walls.

Her eyes are closed. Her back is curved off the bed. She squirmin' like she can't get enough of this dick.

Fuck it. Head or not. Delia is a pretty bitch and I like the way she fuck. This bitch got my heart racin' and sweat drippin' off my body.

She says it's been a long time since she fucked somebody just because she wants to. Well, we got somethin' in common, 'cause it's been a minute since I fucked a bitch without gettin' *somethin'* out of it.

"Come on, Rhak," she begs, her voice whinin' and shit while she lift her hips up and then down to make her pussy pull on my thick dick. "*Fuck* . . . me."

I look down in her eyes as she brings her hands up to massage her own nipples as she makes one of her eyebrows arch up like she darin' me to tear that pussy up.

Humph.

I get on my knees, grab her skinny thighs, and put one of her legs on each of my shoulders. "You ready for this?" I ask her before I lick her ankles.

"Yes . . . yes . . . yes."

Okay, she back to *that* shit again.

I drop my hands to her ass and squeeze them cheeks

close, makin' the pussy clamp down tighter on my dick. I give her three hard pumps. *BAM! BAM! BAM!*

She gasps.

I give her three more. *BAM! BAM! BAM!*

I feel her pussy get warmer. Wetter. A little looser.

I like it. I like it a lot.

Fast and deep I throw my hips, makin' my dick tap the bottom of that pussy until it's talkin' to me. Tellin' me how good my dick is with every smack of her juices. Tellin' my dick is hard with each slap of my thighs against her ass. Tellin' me to fuck it harder with each grunt from her lips.

I fuck her fast like a drum roll. *Pow-pow-pow-pow-pow-pow-pow-pow-pow-pow-pow-pow!*

She starts breathin' like she tryna swallow air.

Pow-pow-pow-pow-pow-pow-pow-pow-pow-pow-pow-pow!

My sweat drips down onto her body while her eyes get big.

Pow-pow-pow-pow-pow-pow-pow-pow-pow-pow-pow-pow!

My heart beatin' like a motherfucker. It's beatin' so loud I can't hardly hear shit else while I look down at her and squeeze her titties so hard I think she gone tear 'em off.

Pow-pow-pow-pow-pow-pow-pow-pow-pow-pow-pow-pow!

I feel like I'm gone catch a cramp but I keep power-drivin' that pussy. I can't stop. I *won't* stop.

She arches her back and grabs at her chest.

Pow-pow-pow-pow-pow-pow-pow-pow-pow-pow-pow-pow!

"Say my name," I tell her, my face twisted from the nut I feel buildin' up.

"Rhak. Rhak. Rhak."

Humph. Two things I know I can do in life is deliver a good fuck and manipulate women.

BOOM! BOOM! BOOM!

I look over my shoulder just as the bedroom door slams back against the wall and Polette is standing there. "You motherfucker, you!" she screams at the top of her lungs.

Delia grabs my ass and pushes me deeper inside her like she sayin' to hell with Polette. "Yes, yes, yes," she moans.

I realize I am still grindin' my hips and slingin' that dick to her. Something about it is freaky as shit and my dick gets harder even as I keep lookin' over my shoulder at Polette.

Delia grunts all soft and shit.

Polette mouth drops wide open.

Even though I'm lookin' at her I still don't know how she got across that floor onto my back so fuckin' fast.

I holler out as she wraps her arms around my neck and starts chokin' the shit out of me. Delia reaches above me and starts deliverin' blows to Polette's head. It's a hell of an ass-whippin' sandwich.

But I'm still pumpin' away in Delia. *Pop-pop.* Fuck it.

"What the fuck?"

Okay, that voice I don't recognize.

"Get the fuck off me," Polette screams.

She's off my back and hands are takin' her arms from around my damn throat. I feel her drag her nails into my back. I look down at Delia and her eyes are big as shit. "Who the fuck is they?" she says, startin' to push me off her with more strength than I thought her little scrawny ass would have.

I feel someone's hands grab my arms and pull me out the bed. For a second Delia's body comes with me like we're attached. I look over my shoulder and those same two detectives who questioned me are standin' there. The black female is holdin' Polette while the big white dude in brown slacks and a striped shirt drenched with sweat is standing by with his hand on his gun.

Now my dick shrivels right on up.

"That's him. That's Rhakmon. Lock his no-good ass up," Polette is screamin'.

"If you don't hold still I'm going to lock *your* ass up," the black female cop tells her in this hard voice.

"Yo, what's goin' on?" I ask as the man puts cuffs on my wrist behind me.

I look left and Polette shoots spit at my face. She misses. Thank God, 'cause Polette breath can get funkier than a motherfucker.

I look right. Delia is standing in the corner holdin' a sheet up to hide her naked body.

"What the fuck is goin' on?" I ask while he hauls me

to my feet with my pants and drawers down around my ankles with my dick swingin' as much as it can while fear fucks me right on up. Hell yeah, I'm nervous as shit and lost like a motherfucker.

Man, what the fuck is goin' on?

22

The Killer

I've lost my religion.

I've lost my way.

That ugly fuck Charlie off C-Block was right about me. I can't dress it up or pass it off. There's a stench on me that I'll never be able to wash off. Killin' my old childhood friend is now a new collection to my nightly nightmares and for a month now I've been tryin' to bury it in the back of my mind.

I no longer pray.

I've stop preachin' on the street corners and I can't even look at my old worn-out copy of the Holy Quran.

I was better off in the joint. Hell, I was better off in that damn Dumpster.

Zoey is pregnant.

After staring at the fifth positive pregnancy test, the shit is finally startin' to sink in. I crouch forward over the bed with my head in my hands. "What the fuck are we goin' to do?" I ask, not really expecting an answer.

"Maybe you can work for Kaseem," Zoey suggests.

"One bust and they'll throw away the key on my ass," I tell her. Of course, neither one of us mentions that's exactly what's gonna happen if I'm ever tied to M. Dawg's murder. But right now, the body hasn't been discovered.

I glance over at her while she drops her head. The bruises on her face and neck are almost gone. To be safe, we stay clear from talkin' about that whole night. It's our own little trick at pretending that it never happened.

"What about that job Sweet offered you? Being a bouncer is a legitimate job."

"You know why that's out of the question."

"Yeah, but you said yourself that he doesn't know that you killed his brother."

I shake my head. "C'mon. You know that would be pretty foul for me to take a job from him whether he knows or not."

"We can't eat pride," she stresses.

My gaze hardened at the familiar words M. Dawg had spoke to me last month. I'm able to put a cap on my anger by turning away.

After a long silence, she tosses up her hands. "Okay. I'm out of suggestions. What do you want to do?"

"Rewind and put a condom on."

She crosses her arms and stares me down. "Seriously."

"How much would it cost if we—"

"I'm past my first trimester. It's much too late for that."

I push off the bed and start pacing the bedroom. "Then fuck it. I'll have to find something."

She bobs her head. "I have a job interview in an hour. Hopefully, I'll get it."

I push on a smile because I know that's what she wants, but what I need is a good damn punching bag.

Zoey rubs her neck. Something she's been doing a lot of lately while I pretend not to notice. One of these days I should make an honest woman out of her. It's the least I can do after the shit I put her through.

"I better go if I want to be on time for that appointment." She turns up a heavy smile and I walk over to reward her with a kiss.

"You still think we're going to be able to make it through this?" she asks.

"Of course we will. You're my Bonnie."

"And you're my Clyde."

"Damn right." I kiss her again and she gets up and heads out the apartment. "Good luck," I tell her, and then head toward the bathroom for a hot shower. It's a good place for me to try and think.

The stash I'd lifted off M. Dawg's ass plus what I was able to get for his ride was enough to pay a few bills, get Tonya's crazy ass off me, and even pay my parole fees.

Now we're flat broke again. I've picked up a few-odd construction jobs but only making about the same money the illegals make—which is hardly any money at all.

Maybe Zoey is right. I should take Sweet up on his job offer. She and M. Dawg are right about one thing: We can't eat my pride. Still, things gotta get a little more desperate before I show my ass up over at Club Diamond.

I shut off the scalding shower and wrap a towel around my hips just as a mad hammering erupts on the front door. "Who the fuck?" I stomp out of the bathroom and about halfway to the door, it occurs to me that it could be the police.

Shit. Maybe they found M. Dawg's body and have come to arrest me. I stop. Think. There are no weapons in this motherfucker and I'm on the second floor where the only other way out is through the window.

"Mr. Jones. Mr. Jones, are you in there?"

My heart pound again at the sound of my parole officer's voice. I open the door. "Ms. Harding?" I glance down the tattered hallway. "What are you doing here?"

Her dark brow climbs toward her blond hairline. "It's customary for parole officers to make house visits." She folds her clipboard in her arms. "Now are you going to let me in?"

I hesitate for a second and then step back.

Ms. Harding comes through the door, glancing around like a health inspector. If I know this bitch like I think I know her, she came over for this house visit for one reason only. As I close the door, I start estimating when Zoey will be back from her job interview.

"Nice place you got here," Ms. Harding says, setting her purse and clipboard down on the coffee table.

"Thanks."

When I fold my arms, her eyes lock on my muscled guns and chest. This is the first time she has seen me this close to naked. The times I fucked her in her office, I didn't do more than just unzip my pants to give her what she wanted.

"Interesting tattoo," she says, reading KILLER etched out across my chest.

I don't say anything, but that doesn't erase her wicked smile. Then her gaze drifts to the wall behind me. "What happened there?"

I turn and see the dented space in the wall where I'd rammed Zoey's head. I wouldn't mind doing the same shit to her. I don't like the position she's put me in, but on the flip side, she's also been pretty lenient about my lack of a steady job and few missed parole fees.

"I don't know," I lie. "It was there before I moved in."

She accepts the lie and returns to looking around—and removing her jacket. "Where's the bedroom?" she asks.

"In the back," I say without moving.

She glances back at me over her shoulder, her smile still in place. "Show me."

My stomach turns at the thought of fucking her hairless, smelly-ass pussy, but I move away from the door and lead the way to the bedroom.

"Ooh, now this is a big bed," she says, sitting her ass

on one corner and bouncing up and down. "I bet you can really do some damage to some pussy on this motherfucker," she says.

Again, I don't answer.

Harding stops bouncing and curls a finger at me. "Stop being all shy and get over here. I've been dreamin' about that fat dick of yours."

"Look. My girl is gonna be home any minute."

"Then you better hurry the fuck up," she says, finally losing her smile.

"Look. People talk around this motherfucker."

"Relax. Nobody saw me come in, I parked down at Hollywood Courts and came in the building through the back after I saw your girl leave."

"You fuckin' stalkin' me or something?"

"Or somethin'," she said, finding her smile again. "What can I say, Killer? You got me whipped. And since I've been more than lenient on your shoddy fee payments and overlooking your inability to maintain a steady job, I figure you wouldn't mind our little arrangement. Am I wrong?"

I glare at her as she unbuttons her shirt. "Now, are we gonna get this shit started now or would you rather have your girl catch us in the act?"

I walk over to the bed with images of me wrapping my hands around her throat flashin' in my head.

Harding whips the towel from around my waist and my cock doesn't bother to salute her dyke-lookin' ass.

"There's that pretty motherfucker," she says as she wraps her fat fingers around my dick and then stuffs it into her mouth as if she hadn't eaten in a week.

My hand instantly falls to the back of her neck as I grind my shit to the back of her throat. Her hands slide and cup my muscled ass cheeks. Okay, the ugly bitch can give some good fuckin' head. I'm strokin' to the back of her tight-ass throat and slappin' my balls against her chin and she's takin' it like a pro.

She stops just as my nut sack tingles and rips out of her clothes. At least today she douched that shit and I have no trouble keepin' my erection hard long enough to work it into her pussy from behind.

She moans as I stretch her soppin' wet pussy but I don't wait for her to get adjusted to my size. I just start pounding away.

I hear her say, "Wait" and "Hold up," but fuck that shit. She wants some motherfuckin' dick, I'm gonna give it to her. "Turn your ass around," I growl, smackin' her on the ass.

She does it without question.

"You really want to see how I get down?" I ask her, crammin' my shit back into her and folding her over like a taco so I don't have to look her in the face. "I'm gonna knock the wall out of this mutherfucker."

In no time at all, the bed is bangin' the floor and slappin' the wall and I'm fuckin' killin' this pussy like it's personally the source of all my problems. At some point, I

Meesha Mink & De'nesha Diamond

unlock her legs so they can fall down around my waist, but my hands are now wrapped around her throat.

"You like this dick, bitch? Huh?" I pound against her with such force that there's a sweet stinging pain when our flesh slaps together. I don't even realize that she can't answer me. I'm squeezin' too tight. "This is what the fuck you came here for, right?"

Her pussy is dryin' up.

"You gonna take this dick. And you gonna fuckin' love it, you hear me?"

I'm chokin' the shit out of her, but I can't let go. Not until I fuckin' bust this nut. Not until I get what's fuckin' comin' to me.

Harding tugs at my hands, but it only angers me. "You wait for this nut, bitch. You wait for it, goddammit."

Finally my shit shoots off and I'm roaring like a damn animal. No shit, it's the best nut I've ever had. I collapse on top of her, panting like I've just raced around the world.

But the body beside me is still.

23

The Dealer

Candy is dead.

I shift in my seat on the front row at the funeral parlor. I try not look at her casket because the woman lying there doesn't look like Candy. Not because of the drugs that claimed her body and her soul but because she lay dead for several days before her body was discovered in an abandoned building.

I think of the money I gave her. The dope I gave her.

Guilt eats at me.

"My baby, Lord why . . . why . . . *WHY* . . . you take my baby?"

I cut my eyes up to where Candy's mother is busy trying to climb into the casket with her daughter. She got a good three hundred pounds packed on her short-ass frame and I'm nervous as shit that the casket gone tip the fuck over and send Candy rolling out like a fuckin' burrito.

Thank God several serious-lookin' dudes from the funeral parlor pull her ass right on out and lead her back to her seat.

I ain't gone lie, it's hard as hell to swallow how Candy died. She *was* somebody I used to love. She *was* the mother of my son.

I turn my head to look down at him sleeping peacefully in my girl's arms. I shift the pants leg of my Gucci pinstripe suit. I want to run out of here. I never liked funerals but here I am. And footing the bill too. Fuck it. It's the least I can do for her for bringing my seed into this world.

And he is the most important thing to me.

At one time I was just as addicted to the game as these heads was to my product. But I'm goin' into my own type of rehab to get away from this shit cold turkey.

A nigga is makin' moves. Plans. Changes. Fuck it.

And I don't mean part-time slingin' while I run a business or handing the business over to Usher the way Maleek put me on to dealin' crack and coke.

I'm already looking into using the money I got to get what the fuck I want. Just like I ran this dope game— *this dope business*—I can run some legit shit. Every hood can use more laundromats. Fly-ass hair salons. Clothing stores. Corner stores. Something. I got to find a new way to make a living because I'm out for good.

My money's going to change like a motherfucker.

The people around me going to change like a motherfucker.

The life I live is going to change like a motherfucker.

I can't explain why I held back from telling anyone. Not Usher. Not my girl. Not my connections. Nobody. I know I have to tell them sooner or later. But I keep pushing it away for later. Every day I feel like it's not that day.

Maybe I'm scared they won't understand.

I made sure these last few weeks to get my shit straight. I don't owe nobody shit and I ain't buyin' more weight.

"This is a sad-ass funeral," Quilla leans over to whisper to me. The scent of her Gucci Rush perfume circles my head. It just a reminder that she loves the finer things in life just like me. The Yves Saint Laurent suit, shoes, and shades she is wearing cost more than this entire funeral.

I'm prepared to downgrade from Gucci to GAP. Is she?

"Hey . . . You okay?"

I look down at her and then at my son and then back at her. She smiles up at me softly and I follow the impulse to lean down and press my lips to her. She tastes like love.

An organist in the corner of the funeral parlor begins to play a soft tune as the fifty or so funeral goers are led up to view the body. Mostly young fellas still dressed in jeans and oversized, colorful polos or females in black skintight club clothes trail by to say good-bye to somebody way too fucking young to die.

I feel a hand on my shoulder and I look up to see the

funeral director ready to lead the row I'm sitting in up to the casket. I clear my throat, straighten my tie, and rise.

Candy is dead. Damn.

I reach for the gold-rimmed aviator shades in the inner pocket of my jacket. I need them because I feel the tears welling up in my eyes. Fuck that. *Knuckle up,* I tell myself.

This shit don't seem real.

Candy is dead.

I turn and take Dashon from Quilla before I walk up to the casket. I can feel the eyes piercing my damn back. If they waitin' on a big dramatic scene they can forget about it. I'm just going to pay my respects and keep it moving. The family is waiting for their turn to say good-bye.

I look down at her lying there so peacefully and I wish I could make our son understand this moment. This is the last time he will be near his mother.

I can't stop the tears that race from my eyes.

I don't stop Quilla from taking him from my arms as I look down at Candy.

People always talking about the game but this shit is about more than the hustle and the hustlers. The game encompasses all. The users. The community.

This. The death. The destruction. This is a part of that game, too.

Humph. Game over.

Click.

I look over my shoulder to see who is walking into the

funeral parlor so late. The double door to the rear of the funeral parlor opens and two masked men walk in with guns pointed forward.

At me.

For two seconds there is a calm.

Then all hell breaks loose.

Women scream as everyone hits the floor or runs out of side entrances just as the gunfire begins.

Pow-pow-pow-pow-pow-pow!

I'm not strapped. I drop down just as bullets fly at me. They hit the casket instead.

Somebody is tryna kill me.

Pow-pow-pow-pow-pow-pow!

"Lord, why, Lord. WHY?" Candy's mother screams at the top of her lungs from her spot behind a potted plant.

I crawl across the floor . . . away from Quilla and my son. If I'm gone die I'm not gone let any bullets fly their way and hit them instead of me. I'll gladly take the bullet first.

Pow-pow-pow-pow-pow-pow!

I watch from the floor as the force of the bullets entering the casket make Candy's corpse move up and down inside it like a jumping bean. I keep crawling across the floor away from everyone else—away from my assassins—but I run into a corner. This is the epitome of a dead end for me. I ain't gone lie. The sounds of police sirens ain't never sound so fuckin' good to a hustler like me.

Hopefully these mark-ass niggas will—

Click.

I look up and one of the gunmen is standing over me with his gun pointed at my chest. My eyes meet his eyes. I see nothing but the desire for my death.

My son will be an orphan. A motherless and fatherless child.

"Noooooooooooo!" I hear Quilla cry out.

I keep my eyes locked on him as I stand to my feet before him. I will die a man. Fuck that.

The sounds of the siren get louder. Closer.

POW! The gun fires and my body jerks back and hits the wall from the impact.

No, I never did any damage with my own hand or my own gun, but I authorized it. I abided it.

When you live by the sword you die by the sword.

24

The Killer

"Oh fuck!"

I scramble off the bed and blink down at the body. When the chest fails to rise and fall, I start to hyperventilate. I can't think. If there was a gun in this muthafucka I'd probably shoot myself. Might as well put myself out of this misery and be done with it.

I pace the bedroom with my dick slappin' my thighs and my muscles coiled into knots. Two mutherfuckin' bodies in two months. What the fuck?

There's a sudden hammering at the door.

"Oh shit. Oh shit." I squeeze my head in between my hands, hoping it will help pop out an idea.

The hammering continues; I have to do something before whoever it is bangs the door down. I rush from the bedroom, closing the door behind me and then find my robe in the bathroom before heading toward the front door.

I peek out the small peephole and damn near roll my eyes to the back of my head. "Go away, Tonya!"

"Nigga, open this door!"

I know she's gonna start a commotion and draw a crowd if I don't do something. I wrench open the door, grab her by the arm, and jerk her inside—almost all in the same motion.

"Nigga, what the fuck do you think you're doin'?"

I slam her up against the wall and lift her off the floor until her head nearly matches Zoey's imprint perfectly. "What the fuck are you doin' here, Tonya?"

She tries to jerk her arm from my gasp. "I'm here for my money, nigga. Let me go."

"I gave you some money last month."

"This is a new motherfuckin' month. I got bills and your son needs to eat. Not that you give a fuck."

"I'll get you your money. You need to stop rollin' up over here. The shit ain't cool."

"What? Am I pissin' off your fat-ass girlfriend?"

My hand tightened on her arm. "You fuckin' watch your mouth."

"Shit. Motherfucker, stop. That hurts."

"That's not all that's gonna hurt if you keep bringin' your sorry ass around here." I smack her into the wall again. Fear creeps into her eyes when I'm two seconds from snapping her arm off.

"All right. All right. I'm sorry," she pants.

"You gonna stay your ass away from here?"

She hesitates a bit too long and I twist a little harder, causing her voice to hike a few octaves. "All right. All right. I won't come by here again."

I plant my face in front of hers, and something about her naked pain gives me another hard-on. "I fuckin' mean it, Tonya. You show your face around here again and it'll be the last motherfuckin' thing you do." I release her and she scrambles out the apartment like a cockroach when the lights come on.

I expel a breath and wipe a line of sweat from my forehead. Now how the fuck am I gonna get a dead body out this motherfucker with those two old biddy posted out front? Shit. They probably saw Harding come into the building.

No. Wait. She said that she came into the building through the back.

Shit. Shit. Think. Think.

There's an empty apartment on this floor. Maybe if I pick the lock I can move the body over there. *But then what?* I ask the voice inside my head.

I can't get a whole body out of here but I can definitely take it out in pieces.

It actually took me seven days to get the last of Ms. Harding out of the empty apartment down the hall. Two more days to clean up the mess. It's a good thing, too. I saw the superintendent go in that motherfucker this morning, checkin' it out for a new resident.

Meanwhile, I keep waitin' for the shit to hit the fan. Zoey thinks I'm just worried about having another mouth to feed and she tries to give me my space. I haven't even touched her in days and when she touches me, I turn away.

But at long last, my pride has to take a backseat when our home phone is turned off. Zoey got that new job, but she's making four dollars less an hour. I drop her off for her first day and then drive the car out to Club Diamond.

From the moment I pull up into the parking lot, I'm impressed. The futuristic white building is shaped like a large boomerang and lined with a four-foot, black wrought-iron gate. The place actually looks like it a high-art museum and as I approach the glass doors, I actually start to get a little nervous. When I open the door, my feet sink into the club's lush black-and-gold carpet with printed blue diamonds while the light scent of strawberries fills the air.

"May I help you?"

I glance up to a long marble counter with an attractive ebony-hued sistah with a sunshine smile and very little clothing. "Yeah, I'm here to see Tavon Johnson about a job. He gave me his card."

"I'm sorry," she said, her cinnamon-painted lips holding onto its smile. "Sweet doesn't come in on Tuesdays. The best times to catch him here are Thursdays, really."

"Oh," I say, and then try to hide my disappointment.

"Thanks, then." I turn and head back out the door, but not before giving the place another quick glance. It's good to know that some niggas were able to escape the bullshit street games and really roll in some long-ass green.

I'm halfway back to Zoey's car when another car rolls up on me.

"Hey. Don't I know you?"

I turn my head toward a sweet champagne-colored Jag. The woman behind the wheel tilts down her black shades. "I don't think so." I scoop the car keys out of my pocket.

"Yeah, I do. You stay in Bentley Manor."

I frown at this chick, wondering what the fuck she really wants.

"Used to run with the Disciples; just got out the pen after serving a dime."

"What the fuck? You writin' a book or somethin', lady?"

"No." She pauses and then adds, "But I might be offering you a job."

That catches my attention. "What kind of job?"

A slow smile curves her lips. "One that pays damn good."

"I'm listenin'."

"How does . . . thirty large sound to you?"

My heartbeat kicks up a notch. "It sound like it's illegal."

"I won't tell if you don't."

I stare at her and realize that this bitch is serious. "I think I'll pass," I say, sliding my key into the door.

"A hundred."

She has my attention again. "A hundred thousand dollars?" I ask for clarification.

"Half now and the other half when you finish the job," she says.

"What's the job?"

"Climb in and I'll tell you all you need to know."

I'm late picking up Zoey from work, but one look at my smiling face, her irritation melts away.

"You got the job at Club Diamond?" she asks, jumping into the car.

"No," I say and then lean over the seat to press a kiss against her lips.

She frowns. "Then why in the hell are you smiling?"

"Because I'm going to take you out on the town."

"What the fuck? You win the lottery or something?"

"You can say that." I shift the car into drive and quickly hit the open highway.

"Don't I even get a hint to what's going on?"

"Open the glove compartment."

She does as she's told and her eyes immediately bug out at the sight of a very large envelope with money bulging out of it. "What the fuck is this?"

"A little sumptin' sumptin' to get us on our feet."

"But—"

"Be careful of what you ask, you might not like the answer."

She clamps her mouth shut and swallows hard.

I smile. "And that's just the down payment."

She gasps and then stares at the money again.

I glance over at her, trying to gauge her feelings at the moment. "Everything is finally comin' together for us, Zoey. This will set us straight."

Zoey is quiet for so long, I don't know what the fuck she thinkin'. I turn off onto our exit and chance another look at her. She's smiling with tears falling down her face.

"You happy, baby?"

She leans over and wraps her arms around me. I nearly steer off the road, laughing. "Watch it, baby. We don't want to wreck your shit."

Zoey ignores me and rains kisses along the side of my face. "I love you. I love you. I love you!"

Damn. She's practically glowing. That shit makes me feel good.

When I park right next to Miz Cleo's long-ass Lincoln, Zoey stuffs the money into her purse and then we climb out the car. Zoey rush into my arms and rain kisses all over my face as we head toward our apartment building.

"Well, you two look like you're in a good mood," Miz Cleo comments, smiling up at us while her great-grandbaby attempts to ride her tricycle again.

"Yeah," Miz Osceola comments. "It's been a while since we've seen you two smiling like that."

"Well, we finally got good reason to," I brag. "Things are finally looking up for us."

Just as soon as I kill one last person.

25

The Pimp

I fuckin' give up.

Renee lied to me.

Destiny fucked my kid.

Now Corrine has run away again. Hell, this time I don't know if I even want her to come back. I'm so sick of the drama swirling around this kid. In the four months I've known her, my life has been turned upside down in a way that I would have never thought possible. It's definitely the reason why I've been smoking a little bit more weed and emptying a few more liquor bottles.

I can take a lot of shit, but betrayal is not one of them. That's stabbing in the back shit—and that's exactly what the two people I trusted the most has done. For peace of mind, I moved out the house and bought a studio not far from Club Diamond. Since I'm not with Renee, Momma has moved in and has made herself right at home.

Of course none of this means that Renee and Destiny haven't been blowin' up my cell phone. On the contrary. That motherfucker has been going off on the regular.

And I've been ignoring each and every call.

In the last month, I've stayed busy by spending my time at the Red Light District studios and/or mingling with the rich and famous while lacing their arms with my hottest Diamond trim. But no matter what I do, my mind keeps tumbling over how fucked up my situation really is.

I miss my wife.

And my best friend.

And even my fucked-up daughter.

That must be the only reason why I finally ride back over to the house on this cold October night. I've been parked outside the crib for a while now, trying to decide on what I'm gonna do. I think back on all the shit Renee and I have been through—all the shit I've put her through—and there's no doubt I that my baby loves me, and that I love her.

It's just this fuckin' trust thing.

"Sir, would you like for me to take you back to your condo?" Anderson asks. His ass is probably tired of sitting out here with my zombie-lookin' ass.

"Nah. I'm gettin' out."

Anderson springs out the car and then rushes to my door and opens it.

I climb out, lean on my silver-headed cane, and dust

off my shoulders. Despite the house being lit up, I really don't know whether Renee is home, but I've convinced myself that it's time to try to squash at least some of this shit between us if we're gonna try to move on.

The minute I enter the house, I can't deny that it doesn't feel good to be home. I cross through the open foyer, head down the hall toward the living room, and pull up short when I catch sight of Renee's silhouette against the ceiling to floor back window. The only light in the room flickers from the fireplace.

I absolutely love the way she fills out her red silk nightgown. It reminds me of another reason why we're still together after all this time.

"It's dark in here."

Renee jerks away from the window and sloshes the drink in her hand. "Sweet," she says with a quivering breath. "You came back."

"Just to talk."

Her smile trembles as she steps forward and weaves awkwardly on her feet.

"You're drunk," I say.

"Just a little bit," she admits. "I thought that you were never comin' back. I thought you and Destin . . ."

She doesn't know what happened between me and Destiny. I haven't been home since that night.

"Sweet, I'm sorry," she says, sitting her glass down and rushing over to me. "I should have never kept something like that from you. Please forgive me. Come back home."

She throws herself into my arms and drenches my shoulder with tears. "I'll do anything. Just please come back home."

I've never been a romantic kind of guy. I always went with what felt good, and Renee has always felt good. Just like she does right now. I brush a kiss against her forehead and she responds by hooking her arm around my neck and dragging my head down for a kiss that nearly sucks my soul right out of me.

Before I know it, I drop my cane and peel her out of that red gown, filling my hands with her firm breasts. I give them a good hard squeeze and pull on the diamond stud pierced through her chocolate nipples.

Renee pulls her lips from mine to suck in a sharp breath while I drop my head to tongue-bathe the center of her body. It's like she's been coated with sugar and I can't get enough. In no time at all, I'm on my knees and sliding her red-laced thong down her luscious hips and I press a kiss against the diamond tattooed above her clit.

This will forever be my pussy.

I move my lips a little to the left and then ease my tongue inside her clit and sap a little of her sweet honey.

Fuckin' delicious.

I dive in again and try to lap up every drop her body has to give.

"Oh, goddamn, Sweet," she pants. Her hands plow into my hair.

I shake my face, tryna get in deeper while sliding two

fingers inside to get to the spots I can't reach. Finally, I just roll down to the floor and then tell her, "Sit on my face."

Like always, Renee waste no time doing what she's told and when she lowers her sopping pussy, she also stretches out toward my crotch to undo my pants and deep-throat my cock.

I glide my hands around her hips and spread her wide open so I can feast like it's Thanksgiving. When her legs start tremblin', I'm prepared for her nut to drench my face. When her orgasm hits, I nearly drown in her syrupy cum.

The head she's giving me feels damn good, but she lacks the jaw power I'm used to with Destiny so I just tell her, "Climb on and ride, baby."

"Hell, yeah."

Renee and I scramble to get me out of my clothes and I damn near cum too damn soon when her wet heat eases down on me. I only have a coupla seconds to get control before she starts winding her hips and flexing her inner muscles.

"Aww, shit." I reach down and cup that luscious ass that I've been fuckin' for more than half my life. "Stop fuckin' around, baby, and ride." From the first bounce my ass is lost. Nobody rides like my baby.

"Am I still your number one girl?" she asks between pants.

I bite my lower lip and feel my toes curl.

"Hmmm, baby? Am I still number one?"

"Awwww. Fuuuuck, yeah!" I start throwin' my hips back at her and poundin' that pussy like it owed me fuckin' money.

"I'm gonna always be number one, right, baby?" she asks.

"Uhmm. Hmmm," I moan, but I really don't give a fuck about what the hell she's sayin'. My nut sack is tingling again and I'm ready to blast off.

"That fuckin' jump-off ain't got shit on this here, baby. You remember that. This pussy is your home," she groans.

"Uhmm. Hmm." I flip her ass over; press her face into the carpet so I can attack this shit from the back. Our bodies slappin' together is the best damn music in the world. Renee is comin' so hard she leaves wet spots all over the carpet.

"I fuckin' love you, Sweet. Don't you ever forget it. Everything I've ever done has been for you, baby." She tightens her inner muscles one last time and my hot shit explodes out the tip of my dick like a popped champagne cork.

I slump forward over her ass and struggle to catch my breath. When air finally flows back into my lungs, I make small bites across her back. "Thanks, baby. I needed that shit." I smack her on the ass and climb back onto my feet in search of my pants.

Renee watches me with a lazy smile until I grab my cane from off the floor. "Wait. Where are you going?"

I walk over to her, lean down, and brush a kiss against her forehead. "You're the best." I turn to leave.

"What the fuck?" I hear her jump to her feet. "What— you just came over to fuck me and now you're leaving? Is that it? I'm just one of your hos on payroll, is that the fuck it?"

I turn and face her. "I came to talk, but I've eliminated some unnecessary stress and I'm ready to roll."

"What the fuck? Nigga, you got some goddamn nerve, strollin' up in here and usin' me like some blow-up god-damn doll. I'm your wife, goddammit! I deserve some fuckin' respect."

"You had that, but you fucked that up, didn't you?"

"Nigga, please. You treat that motherfuckin' he/she better than you do me, you goddamn faggot."

In two strides I'm back in front of her and knockin' the damn taste out her mouth.

When she rocks her head back onto her neck, she glares at me with blood tricklin' from her busted lip. "What— beatin' my ass is gonna make you feel more like a man?" She holds out her arms. "Then have at it, because you're gonna hafta be at it all night to knock the rest of that sugah out yo tank."

For the first time with Renee, I crash my fist across her jaw instead of using my backhand. The blow knocks her off her feet. "You done lost yo rapid-assed mind, poppin' off at the mouth with me like that! Last time I checked, your ass ain't all that particular on who's runnin' up in your shit either, or did you forget that your ass is just one notch above the rest of these hos I stick my dick in?"

She sobs, clearly heartbroken.

"I'm gettin' the fuck out of here, before you make me do something I'ma regret." I turn and take two steps before her liquor glass whiz pass my head and smash against the living room wall.

"Go ahead," she screams. "Go back to your fuckin' freak. Enjoy his ass while you can! His fuckin' time is up!"

My heart stops as something cold slithers down my back. "What the fuck did you say?"

She tilts her chin up defiantly and gives me a smug look.

"What the fuck did you do?" I rush back toward her and grab her ass. "I'm gonna ask you one more time: WHAT—THE—FUCK—DID—YOU—DO?"

Renee's wicked laugh fills my ears. "I erased his ass!"

26

The Dealer

Thank God I'm alive.

My chest hurt like a bitch from the bullet but thankfully it missed anything major and just passed straight through my body. I bled like a fucking hog but surgery was able to get it patched back up.

Looking at death got a nigga's head straight these last couple of weeks. For one, I stay strapped. All that partyin' and poppin'-bottle shit is on pause. I got a son to raise and I ain't gone let these streets take me the fuck out. I wince as I turn the steering wheel of this bullshit-ass black '69 Chevy Nova—newly done with bulletproof windows. Fuck that. A nigga is on the low for sure. Right now everybody think I'm in New York handling business. Well, they thought wrong. I turn into Bentley Manor and park in front of the first building on the left.

The lot is mainly empty. It's cold as hell in Georgia

during an October night. That cut down most of the traffic around this motherfucker. Good. I just need to get in that apartment, pick up a stash of cash I keep there and the last of the dope I got.

I pull my semiautomatic from the gun holster I'm wearing under my thick, three-quarter-length black leather trench. I make sure the clip is full and tighten the silencer. Fuck that; I'm locked and loaded.

I ain't no killa but don't push me.

This bullshit, this game I used to love, got me away from my son. I don't feel like him and Quilla are safe around me until I find who the fuck want me dead. So Dashon is staying at my parents. He's already been too close to death. I had Usher take Quilla to one of her cousins staying in Vine City.

I throw up the hood and squeeze out this little motherfuckin' car. Going incognegro is a bitch.

But dying is way worse.

I walk in the building and jog up the stairs to the second floor, making sure no one sees me. The hall is empty. I walk into the apartment and hold the door to keep it from closing. Just like I told Olive, she done start packin' up the little bit of shit I had in there. I told her she could have it—.

CLICK.

I freeze as I feel the cold metal pressed behind my ear. I close my eyes and drop my head a little. Damn.

"Why, Usher?" I ask without even turning around.

He laughs a little as he reaches inside my coat to take my gun. My eyes lock on him as he points both guns at me as he circles to stand in front of me. "Why?" he asks again, his bulldog face mocking.

My eyes dipped down to his glassy eyes and the slight streak of white powder by his nose. I had no idea that it was my best friend betraying me until that very moment. No one but him knew I wasn't out of town. No one but him knew I was coming here tonight.

This shit is so fucking cliché and I still missed it. The only thing to really wrap a bow on this bullshit is—

"Why ask why, baby?"

I'll be damned.

My eyes shift to the right and I feel relief. I actually thought it was Quilla's voice I heard. But my eyes still get wide to see first one and then the other of the twins walk out of the bedroom in nothing but matching gold thongs with money—probably *my* money—in their hands.

I watch as they walk over to Usher and he wraps his beefy arms around their waist and pulls each one close to kiss their glossy lips. His hands drop down possessively to lightly smack his guns against their juicy asses. Somewhere along the line, they added tattoos of their names to their dimpled butts.

I don't love these tricks. Hell, they're not Quilla, but I'm still surprised as hell to see these two dimes lappin' Usher's ugly ass like he's the second coming of Jesus. Still, they was on my list of easy pussy and I really don't give a fuck if they give the pussy to Usher.

Right now my best friend is showing me he is my worst enemy. Pussy is the last motherfuckin' thing on my mind.

Suga laughs and leans back to jiggle her titties before she throws the money into the air to rain down on them like confetti. "Big Daddy sick of you and your goody-two-shoes bullshit. It's time for some new blood to run these streets," she purrs as she cuts her eyes over to look at me.

Big Daddy? New blood?

What the fuck ever.

Spyce gently pushes out of Usher's embrace and struts over to me where I stand in the dimly lit living room. "You thought we was just like all them hos you done run through, huh?" she spits at me, her eyes filled with anger. She reaches up and slaps me hard.

I step forward to yoke her ass up.

"Oh no," Usher says, stepping forward with one barrel pointed at my head and the other one at my chest.

I fall back.

Suga takes one of the guns from Usher's grasp with a deep kiss to his lips before she steps up next to her twin and laughs. Her hard nipples are pointed at me as she puts her free hand on her hip and taps her Gucci sandal against the black tiled floor. "You shoulda killed his ass the way we planned," she tells Usher over her shoulder as she curls her glossy lips at me.

My eyes shift to Usher and he just cocks his head and looks at me like "What?" I nod like it's all cool but deep down I can't lie that I'm hurt like a motherfucker. I'm hurt and I'm angry. I'm afraid that tonight is the last night of my life.

One of the twins steps closer to me and puts her hand on my shoulder. She looks up at me before she presses her lips to mine.

"Suga!" Usher roars.

"I'm Spyce," she purrs, as she cocks her perfectly plucked eyebrow and knees me in the nuts. Pain worse than the gunshots radiates from my groin across my whole body. I bend over and grab my shit as she laughs at me. I feel something with an edge roughly pushed against the back of my knees. She brings her elbow down onto the middle of my back.

"That's for not buying my sister them stilettos she wanted, nigga."

Spyce pushes me down into the chair behind me and I have to fight the urge not to bum-rush this bitch and beat her ass. But I'm so aware of the guns locked on me. Usher shot me once. Fuck that. I don't doubt he'll do it again.

Right now it has to be about brain over brawn. I don't have a choice.

Suga or Spyce raises her leg to kick my side viciously. "That's for that abortion you made me have, pimpin'."

That's Suga for sure.

I bite my lip to keep from crying out as she punches my gunshot wound like her ass is going for a knockout.

"Aaah!" I holler out, unable to stop the show of pain.

Usher laughs.

"And this is for thinkin' that bitch Quilla is better than us."

WHAP!

A slap to my jaw. I taste my own blood fill my mouth.

They squat down on either side of me and I can smell that familiar sweet scent of their pussy rise up. *Humph,* right now I'd like to fuck these bitches with a gun and blast off with more than cum.

One makes two fists and starts delivering blow after blow after blow to my face and head while the other one holds the gun on me. Her curses punctuate every fucking lick.

"Punk."

"Pussy."

"Trick."

"Bitch."

My body is aching from the beating this bitch givin' me. My gunshot wound is throbbin' like a bitch. This bitch throws like a fuckin' dude.

"Tie that bitch-ass nigga up," Usher orders them.

Both women freeze and give each other a long sarcastic look before they do as he told them.

My eyes shut as I wince in pain. I hear their heels hit

the tile as they walk away from me. "Usher, this a bunch of bullshit," I tell him, fighting like hell not to give in and pass out from the pain.

I'm still trying to wrap my mind around Usher betraying me and plotting with these trick-ass bitches. For what? Money? Power? Respect?

I open my eyes just as one of the twins walks back over to me with colorful Gucci scarves. She roughly jerks my arms behind my back to tie them. "Now sit your ass here and don't fucking move, you stupid bitch-ass nigga."

Usher is in the background placing every bit of his thick tongue down the other twin's mouth. "It's time for the real king to run these fuckin' streets. Fuck that, we makin' power moves, baby," he shouts to the ceiling once the kiss is thankfully broken.

He grins, looking like a fucking gorilla.

Dumb shit is they ain't had to go through all this shit to run the game. My ass was out and all he had to do was step in. Usher dumb as fuck and I know he just followin' these bitches' lead.

"How long y'all had this shit planned?" I ask the one still squatting behind me.

"Shut the fuck up," she says all quiet and serious.

"Let me go and I'll give you a hundred grand," I offer them.

She sucks her teeth and turns her head to watch her twin bend over in front of Usher with the gun still in her hands as she gives him a booty shake. He smacks her jiggling ass with his gun. "It's time, Suga," she calls over to her sister.

Spyce reaches behind her to pull her thong to the side. Usher rubs her pussy with the barrel until it is slick and wet from her juices. "Come on in this bedroom and let me get this pussy," he tells her.

"No, fuck me right here, Daddy," she moans, jiggling her ass again as she reaches down to pick up the bills scattered under their feet. She reaches between her legs to pat her pussy with the fanned-out bills.

Usher reaches behind him to sit down his gun on the black dining room table. He pulls a vial out his pocket before he drops his pants and boxers. I close my eyes because looking at Usher's dick ain't on my fucking to-do list.

Still I caught a glimpse and what Usher lacks in looks he makes up for in dick. He had a porno-star dick and I have to sit there and watch him pour coke from that vial along the length of that monster before he slides it inch by inch into Spyce.

Suga stands up and walks over to them to take the gun from Spyce's hands as she looks me dead in the eye the whole time Usher fucks like he's punishing her. She didn't flinch from them deep thrusts once. "His dick is so good," she moans like a pro while Usher slides his dick out of her pussy and into her asshole just like that. She moans again and licks her fingertips before she teased her own nipples.

Who the fuck is these motherfuckers I thought were my friends?

"D-d-d-damn, your p-p-p-pussy good, Suga," Usher stutters as sweat pops off his head like raindrops on a roof.

CLICK.

"*I'm* Suga, you ugly motherfucker."

Usher's eyes widen as the bullet tears through his forehead and splatters his brains against the wall behind him. Seconds later he convulses like crazy and then falls to the floor.

Suga blows the end of the gun she is holding as Spyce rises to her full height. "Why you ain't shoot that nigga sooner?" Spyce asks as she snaps her thong back in place with a long acrylic nail before she bends down to take Usher's gun from his hand.

Suga just shrugs.

They both turn and look down at me.

"Everything going just as planned," Suga says.

"*Almost* everything." Spyce walks over to me and brings the butt of the gun down onto the side of my head.

The last thing I see is blood pooling around Usher's head on the floor.

27

The Playa

If looks could kill I would drop Shaterica where she sat. The desire to slap her made my hand itch as I try to sit cool as I can in my chair in the courthouse. I just fold my hands together on top of the wooden defendant's table.

During her entire time on the stand her head hung low with her chin damn near sitting on her chest. I know it's 'cause I was watchin' her closely. Shee-it, I knew it was too late for her to change everythin' her snitch ass done told the police but my eyes were darin' her to do it in my face. "Shaterica, why did you lie to Detectives Lewis and Clayton about shooting and killing Onthario Williams?"

I lick my lips and shift my hand to wipe my mouth smoothly.

"Ms. Drayton?"

Shaterica raises her head, wipes away the tears she was

hidin', and looks right at me. "He tricked me into think-ing that it was better for us if I turned myself in for the murder. He has a record and he said because I didn't I would get way less time."

"And why did you agree?"

"Because I love him," she admits in a whisper just as one tear races down her cheek.

I shift in my seat and lock my fingers on top of the table again. It's my turn to look away from her. I refuse like a motherfucker to call what I feel guilt.

"These are statements from ten Bentley Manor resi-dents but I want you to read the highlighted portion from the statement of Osceola Washington."

So them old birds did stick they nose deep in my shit. That's what all that riddle-ass talk was about that day. *Humph.* I look over my shoulder and sure 'nough, they sittin' they ass right there on the back row enjoyin' every fuckin' minute of my shit catchin' up with me. They have the nerve to wave at me and smile like they just won the fuckin' Georgia state lottery or some shit. I'd give anythin' to flip them bitches the bird but I know all eyes are on this playa for real.

I turn forward as Shaterica, still dressed in her prison uniform, accepts the papers handed to her. I want to pop my knuckles but I play it cool.

Not that it matters. My public defender already hipped me that Shaterica told the police where I hid the gun and my fingerprints are on it. In return for her testimony against me, they are appealing to a judge to have her conviction overturned.

I cock my head to the side as Shaterica licks her lips and holds the papers. The courtroom is quiet as a motherfucker and my fucking stomach feels like I can shit water.

"Rhakmon Reynolds was not only dating Shaterica, he was living with her at Bentley Manor, driving her car, and letting that poor girl take care of his no-good loafing and lying behind." Shaterica stopped. The papers in her hand started to shake and anyone could see she tryin' like hell to get her shit together.

"Now please read this highlighted portion from a brief interview of Mr. Reynolds by the detectives when they asked him—as they did other Bentley Manor residents— if he knew you."

Shaterica shifts her wide frame in the seat and I know only one third of all that ass is actually on the chair. She takes the new set of papers handed to her and licks her lips some more. "Shaterica? Naw, I don't know that fat bitch . . ."

Her voice is just a fucking whisper and I can't lie. I hear the pain and shame all up in it.

"Please continue."

Her face is a mask of pain as one and then two tears race down her cheek. I keep my face the same as she continues to read the words I already know I said. "I see her in passing but I don't know her like that. I don't know why somebody told you that lie about us fucking around. That big bitch ain't even on my fucking level—"

Shaterica drops the papers from her hands. "When the detectives read me his statement I knew he used me up and threw me away. I feel so stupid. I can't believe I wanted to be loved so bad that I was willing to do ten years so he could be free. All because he lied and said he would marry me in the end. I knew he should do his own time. He played me. He used me. He used me. *HE USED ME!*"

She pounds her chest with her finger and the anger is there but suddenly her head drops to her chest as she starts to cry the most pitiful fuckin' cry ever. Her whole body shakes and she reaches to hug herself as she rocks back and forth and cries like a baby.

"He used me," she whispers again and again through the snot and tears.

Regrets? Do I have any?

Hmmm. I gots plenty. Sittin' in this jail for the last month gave me a lot of time to think. Life is what I made it.

Unfortunately for me . . . it is what it is.

I try to get comfortable on the cot readin' old-ass issues of *King, Vibe, XXL,* and *Source,* tryna pretend like my ass ain't in jail. This is the hell I tried to avoid. Your mind ain't got shit to do but reminisce. And that's a lot of shit a nigga like me is tryna forget.

Hustlin' women helped get me in this motherfucker. I

done hustled 'til I can't hustle no fuckin' more. At night I think of all them bitches. All of 'em fuckin' with me in my dreams. Chasin' me. Payin' me back. Alisha. Felisha. Tonya. Evette. Wahida. Monique. Tara. Louisa. Maria. Farrah. Khadijah. Taira. Big Butt Belinda. Deep Throat Delia. Polette. Even that thief Sha-Sha.

Shaterica.

One thing about it. I done had enough pussy to last me the years I might have to spend in this sexless motherfucker.

"Reynolds! Visitor."

I look up at the skinny guard who still wouldn't be no bigger than a buck-ten soakin' wet with boots and a ten-pound weight on.

"Move it!" he hollers, bangin' his club against the metal door.

He ain't fuckin' with nobody but me since I ain't had no cellmate. Thank God. County jail is equal to hell.

I drop the *King* magazine with Meghan Good's sexy ass on the cover. That motherfucker still had nut stains from my last cellmate who got released and did me a favor by leavin' the magazines.

I roll off the bed but I stand back from the electronic door the way we were trained. As soon as it opens the guard puts his hand on his club and motions with his head for me to stroll. I ain't excited because this time of the night it ain't nobody but my bullshit-ass public defender.

Who else gone come see me?

My momma been dead.

My daddy unidentified.

All I ever had to give my bitches was my dick. Well, ain't none of them birds checkin' for a dick on lockdown, so they done move the fuck on. Shee-it, I called Polette collect and that bitch accepted just to tell me to suck a dick and call it Rick 'cause she was more than through with my trickin' ass.

I shake off the tears that burn the back of my throat. I don't give a fuck. I don't need nobody. *Nobody.*

"Whaddup, fish."

I ignore the whispers and kissin' sounds coming from one of the cells we pass. Fuck what you heard, it's some punks up in this bitch. But I fuck, I don't get fucked. And I damn sure ain't gettin' fucked over. I'll catch another case before I let a nigga use me for some ass.

The guard opens the door leadin' to the visitation room. I'm shocked as hell to see Shaterica and some black lady in a suit sittin' there.

Ain't neither one of them on my visitation list. Hell, nobody on that motherfucker.

Shaterica looks up at me and I can tell she got a lot of shit she want to say or to ask me. She wants to feel better. She wants me to admit I'm wrong and apologize.

Obviously someone feels the same way for them to arrange this special visit for her ass. I notice she is in street clothes and not this prison bullshit I'm stuck in. She free.

I think about all my regrets while I'm standin' here lookin' at her. I think of what I should have done better. *Humph.*

I regret like a motherfucker I didn't pick a better bitch to take that wrap for me. *That's* what the fuck I regret.

I gave her an up-and-down look before I turn back to the door. "No visit."

"Rhak," Shaterica calls out behind me.

I ignore her ass. Man, fuck her.

"Rhak, why did you lie, Rhak? I loved you and you used me. You fucking played me."

The door opens and the guards let me back into the hall. I'm happy as a motherfucker when the door shuts out her voice. Fuck all that yellin' bullshit.

I follow the guard back to my cell and my face is mean. Why the fuck they waste my time with *that* bullshit? She wanted some big-time final scene like a fuckin' movie or some shit. Well, I'm sorry, but I ain't gone be able to do it.

She free, now get the fuck on.

I pause when the door to my cell opens and I see a big seven-foot dude with all these fuckin' muscles arrangin' his pillow on the bunk above me. I hear the guard behind me snicker.

What the fuck is this shit all about?

He looks over his shoulder at me from my head to my feet. I could swear that nigga licked his lips and smiled.

The door shuts behind me.

BOOM!

A door ain't never sounded so shut.

"I'm King." His voice is all deep and shit like he talkin' through rocks and fuckin' boulders. "What's your name . . . *fish?*"

Uh-oh.

The lights click out and I step back as he steps forward. I open my mouth to holler out but his large salty hands clamps down over my fuckin' mouth as he picks me up and walks deeper into the cell. Deeper into the fuckin' darkness.

My heart beatin' and I want to fight him but he got one arm around my whole body and I can't move as he licks my earlobe. "Damn, you fine," he whispers.

My damn dick shrivels up like a raisin. I feel nauseous.

My eyes get big as shit as he presses my back against the wall using just one arm to hold my mouth and to pin me. I holler like a bitch against his hand and tears fill my eyes as he jerks my fuckin' pants and boxers down to my knees. I try to kick him away but he takes his hands from my mouth just long enough to slap the shit out of me . . . two times.

WHAP-BAP!

The tears fall as I feel him bend down to take my dick into his mouth. This big muscular motherfucker moanin' and hummin' like a bitch while I wish I could die to keep this big fag motherfucker off me.

Vomit fills my throat and some spills out the sides of his hand as I tremble against that cold wall and pray that he stops. I feel nauseous from the wet feel of him slurpin' on my dick. I don't give a fuck, my dick *ain't* gettin' hard.

Eventually he caught the fuck on and took one last suck to my tip. *Slurp!*

"Dick won't get up," he whispers in my ear when he jerks my body back close to his big sweaty body. He turns me around until my back is pressed to his front. He grinds his hard dick against my buttocks. "That's all right, mine is, *fish.*"

My heart beatin' so hard and I feel like my ass gone pass out. I close my eyes and struggle against him but my strength ain't shit up against his. He bends our bodies as he kneels on the floor and presses me down across my bunk. I squeal against his hand as he slaps my bare ass before he squeezes and rubs it like it's a tittie or some shit.

I squeal like a bitch again when he spreads my ass cheeks and hawk spits on my hole.

"Oh God, please . . . no . . . please. I swear I don't deserve this. Please God . . . please." I pray and I pray as I cry and I cry.

Just as I feel him workin' the tip of his dick into my ass I see an image of Shaterica cryin' so pitifully on the stand.

Damn.

28

The Killer

K-I-L-L-E-R

I can't pull my eyes from the black ink scrawled across my chest. My curse. My brand. My fate.

It's been four and a half months since I walked out of Jesup Federal and it's time for me to accept the hard-ass truth: I'm a fuckin' killer. Killing comes natural for me. It's easy. And truth be told: that last time I fucked my parole officer and squeezed the life out of her, it was the best fuckin' orgasm I ever had.

"Baby, you a'ight in there?" Zoey's voice drifts through the bathroom door.

I open it and flash a smile. "Never better, baby." I walk out of the bathroom, plant a kiss on her full lips, and give her a good whack on the ass.

She jumps with a hard laugh and then follows me to the bedroom as I get dressed.

When I pull out my new all-black gear, she crawls up onto the bed and crosses her legs Indian-style. "Tonight's the night?"

"Yeah." I pull a thin, black turtleneck over my head.

"Is it a drug drop?"

"Zoey." My eyes flash a warning.

"Sorry." She drops her head. "I'm just nervous." To prove it, she crosses and uncrosses her arms. "I'm just trying to figure out what kind of job pays fifty Gs off the tip."

See. I shouldn't have told her about the other half of the money comin'. "Don't worry about it. Whatcha don't know can't hurt you."

"Still . . ."

"Zoey. Let it be."

She bobs her head and flashes a nervous smile. In the past coupla weeks, we've put the advance money to good use. We paid off bills and even set Tonya's ass straight for a little while. When I finish this job and pick up the last fifty G, ends will be meeting like a motherfucker. Hell, we can even go ahead and roll up out of this dirty-ass complex.

For the past week, Zoey has brought home a stack of apartment-hunting guides and has found a nice little apartment complex out in the suburbs; we can pay the lease for a full year and then just start livin' like regular people.

I move over to the bed and pull on my black combat

boots. I really do feel like I'm about to head out to war. All that's missing is a pair of dog tags and a helmet.

"I don't know," Zoey says, drawing in a deep breath. "I'm startin' to have a bad feelin' about all of this."

I close my eyes and exhale a long breath. I was afraid of this. I clap my hands together and lean them against my lips as if in prayer. "Baby, trust me. This is easy money. After tonight, there won't be no duckin' and dodgin' bill collectors, smellin' pissy-ass hallways and battlin' cockroaches for leftovers. We're finally goin' to do this shit—get the fuck up out of here and never look back."

She looks like she's afraid to believe me. I pull her into my arms and draw in a deep whiff of her Wind Song perfume. At last, her arms slide around me. For the first time in four and a half months, I truly feel like her man again. I'm handlin' shit. I'm runnin' this show and it's about time I get paid for doin' what comes naturally to me.

I stand up and walk to the closet and remove the hot piece I picked up down off Langford Parkway last week.

Zoey sucks in another breath. She knows if I'm even pulled over for a traffic violation with this motherfucker, I ain't comin' back home anytime soon.

"Do you really need that?" she asks.

"Protection," I lie and give her another kiss.

She smiles up at me like a beam of sunshine. "You be careful, baby."

"You can count on it."

We walk out of the bedroom together and into the living room where the local news is on.

Police authorities are still looking into the disappearance of Atlanta parole officer, Marsha Harding. It's been nearly three weeks since anyone has seen her. Her abandoned 2002 white Ford Explorer was discovered at Hollywood Courts apartment complex west of Atlanta . . .

I hit the power button as I pass by and then stop at the door to give Zoey another kiss and a reassuring smile. "I love you, baby. I'll be back in a little while."

She nods. "I love you, too. I'll wait up for you."

Seems like she's always waiting for me. We kiss again and then I disappear into the night.

I've cased this million-dollar Buckhead Lake home more than a few times in the past few weeks. If this is how Tavon treated his bottom bitch, then his wife must really be livin' large. Maybe I should've gone into the pussy business.

I find a nice spot about a mile down from Lake Oconee and hiked my way through the dense trees in the dark and up to the house. What makes this job even easier is that my employer has even managed to get me a key to the bottom back door.

Yep. This is the easiest hundred Gs I've ever made in my life. As I make my way from the bottom floor, which is apparently some kind of entertainment room, up to the main floor, I'm as silent as a cat and calm, cool, and collected for what I'm about to do.

The fuse box takes a little work gettin' to, but I manage it and plunge the entire house into darkness. Now there's nothing left for me to do but to sit tight and wait.

Time seems to stretch on forever while my ears strain to hear the slightest sound: the winding moan of the settling foundation, the soft whirl of the heating system, and even the steady pound of my heart.

Twenty minutes feels like an hour and an hour feels like eternity. I nod off a coupla times and when I jerk awake I'm momentarily confused as to where I am. This might be an easy job, but it's also one boring-ass job as well.

Another hour passes and I give serious thoughts to whether this chick is even comin' home. What if she decides to crash somewhere else tonight? I'll have to trek my ass all the way up here again tomorrow.

"Fuck," I mumble under my breath. Just thinking about having to go through all this shit again tomorrow night makes my temples throb.

At long last, I hear a car pulling up the drive.

I smile into the darkness. "Showtime." I reach for my gun and crack open the closet.

"Aww, hell. What the hell happened to the lights?" A female's voice whines in irritation. Then, "Shit," when she bumps into something.

The front door slams and then I hear the click of heels against the hardwood floor.

"This is just great," I hear her say, a second before she passes by my hiding space.

That familiar calm settles over me and I feel as if I'm in my element. I lift the gun to my lips for a kiss before I ease open the door wider. One advantage, my eyes have already adjusted to the darkness and I can see what my target can't while she continues to bump into furniture.

"Goddammit," she swears.

I extend my arm and take aim. "Sorry, lady," I say and watch her whirl around to the sound of my voice. "Rest in peace."

I fire two shots.

She's dead before she hits the floor.

I step out of the closet, remove the flashlight from my back pocket, and quickly stroll over to the body to double check for a pulse. As I approach, I'm amazed at how small she is.

I kneel and roll her over. When the beam of the flashlight hits her face, I suck in a stunned breath. "What the fuck?" This chick is a kid. She can't be more than fourteen or fifteen. Studying her face, I'm hit with a sense of déjà vu. I know this face.

The front door opens again.

"Goddamn, Corrine. What the hell is goin' on with the lights in here?"

I jump up as another figure storms into the living room and sees me holding the flashlight.

The feminine voice drops into a deep bass. "What the fuck?" She drops her bags, but before she can do much else, I lift the gun and fire off two more shots.

This time, the body jumps back and hits the wall, slides down, and then crumples onto the floor.

Amazingly, I'm still calm as I head over to the second dead body. This time when my flashlight settles on the victim's face, I feel a rush of relief.

I've completed my job.

I smile. Now all I have to do is blaze this mutherfucka up and collect my other fifty Gs.

29

The Pimp

"That's right, nigga! I erased your bottom bitch!" Renee spats into my face. "I told you I'd always be number one up in this mutherfucker and I meant that shit."

Rage, fear, and whole lot of other fucked-up emotions boiled in my veins while my mind races with all the possibilities her words implied. "You've gone too far," I growl, digging my fingers into her arms.

"What? You gonna start cryin' about losin' your pet freak?" She tries to snatch herself out my grasp, but her ass ain't goin' no fuckin' where. "Aww. C'mere and let Momma kiss it and make it all better."

Fuck it. I crash my fist back across her jaw and send her sprawling into the carpet. "Whatever the fuck you did, you fuckin' call it off. RIGHT. FUCKIN'. NOW."

Renee just starts laughin' and stretches across the carpet like she's perfectly happy to lay her ass there all night.

I walk over and snatch her head up by her hair. "I mean it, Renee. Call it off."

"Fuck you," she spits back at me. "I ain't doin' a mutherfuckin' thing but lay my ass up in *my* house and call me over a *real* man to fuckin' satisfy me."

This fuckin' bitch wants me to kill her. That shit is clear. If she's done what I think she's done, she might just get her wish. I reach over and grab her red nightgown from off the floor, snatch Renee's drunk ass up, and then proceed to drag her across the living room kicking and screaming.

"Let me go, motherfucker! Let me go!"

When we bust out of the house and into the night, I see Anderson walking across the lawn toward the service quarter.

"Anderson, get the fuckin' car!"

He jumps and races back across the lawn.

Renee kicks and thrashes on the front steps of the house. "Let me go, you weak-ass-dirty-Superfly son of a bitch!"

She finally gets a good clamp on my arm and sinks her teeth deep until it feels like she'd hit bone.

"Aaargh!" I, in turn, kick the shit out of her.

I can't explain my emotions. Yes, Destiny and I are a wrap and yes, I'd come close to killing her myself, but don't none of that mean that I can erase our history. What Destiny meant to me.

Bottom line: This is all fucked up.

Anderson whips the Bentley up to the front of the house like he's the getaway driver of a bank heist and I'm still pulling and tugging Renee's naked ass across the front porch. Finally, I bend down and wrestle to pick her up.

"Fuck you, motherfucker! I'll kill you, too, goddamm it!"

Anderson opens the back door with his eyes wide as fuck. "D-do you need any, uhm, help with that-er-her, sir?"

"Grab her legs and help me get her in the car."

Anderson rushes to do what he's been told; but when he goes to scoop up Renee's feet, she delivers a swift kick across his jaw.

"Get the fuck away from me," she screams; her hands grab hold of the side of the door in a late attempt not to get into the car, but it just takes another backhand for her to tumble inside.

I throw the red gown in after her. "Cover yourself." I look up to Anderson, who is still cradling his jaw. "Take us to the lake house."

"Yes, sir." He races to the driver's seat.

I climb into the car, pushing and shoving Renee to the other side of the seat.

Renee isn't done fighting. She launches toward me with fists flying. "I hate you. I hate you. I hate you." She actually lands a few solid blows and I struggle to ward off the rest of them while simultaneously ducking my head down near her bouncing titties.

One punch she lands across my face was powerful

enough to jerk my head back into a red rage. The blow I land this time sends her head smacking into the passenger window.

She slumps down, panting and clearly jarred.

I touch my lips and see that I'm bleeding. If it was any other woman, the back of this expensive-ass car would have become a homicide crime scene.

Suddenly, she breaks down crying and I can't say I'm unaffected. I had a feeling this love triangle would come to a head one day, but I'd never envisioned this shit.

Panting, I flip through a few compartments and find some tissue to dab the blood on my face. This whole damn thing is just bullshit. I scoop out my cell phone and start calling every number I have for Destiny. I have to tell him what my dumb-ass wife has done.

"Why?" she croaked, crying. "Why do you fuckin' love him so much?" She draws in a ragged breath. "Why can't I be enough for you?"

I turn away from her while a recorded message tells me that all circuits were busy and to try my call later.

"Please. Just tell me why," she sobbed.

I wish I had an answer for her.

About two miles out, the cell phone lines musta cleared because my phone suddenly rings, saving me from Renee's continued pity party. I glance at the screen, not recognizing the phone number.

"Yeah, who is this?"

"I thought you were supposed to be watching our daughter?" Tracy snaps.

I roll my eyes. I really don't have time for this. "What? Is she with you?"

"Who the fuck is that crying?"

"Mind your business. Look, I can't talk right now. If Corrine is with you, keep her there 'til the morning. I'll be by to pick her up."

"That's just it, Daddy Dearest. She's not here with me. I just got some message on my phone telling me that she's movin' in with some guy named Destin."

My heart drops. Corrine is at Destin's with a damn killer on his way there. I disconnect the call with Tracy still throwin' a hissy fit and reach down to the compartment where I keep my 9.

Renee finally shuts the fuck up and manages to move farther away from me. "What the fuck are you about to do?"

I glance up at Anderson and see he's equally nervous. "Corrine is at Destin's tonight," I tell Renee more calmly than I feel.

It's soft, but I hear her gasp.

Slowly, I turn toward her again. "If something happens to my daughter, you're a marked-ass bitch."

I keep callin' Corrine and Destiny's cell phone numbers the rest of the way to the house. Every time I was transferred to voice mail. The car is quiet; Renee has definitely sobered. Once she learned Corrine's life was stake, she spilled her gut about hiring Demarcus Jones out of Bentley Manor for a hundred Gs. I know Demarcus even though we never socialized in the same circles, but I remember hearing that he was a cold motherfucker back in the day.

And to think I offered that nigga a job.

The lake house finally comes into view and I know shit ain't right from the jump because there's not a single light on in the place. I open the door before Anderson comes to a complete stop.

"Tavon, maybe you shouldn't go in there," Renee calls out behind me.

I couldn't turn back now. I have one moment of panic before I kick in the door. I mean, I'm a pimp not a gang-banger. I'm not cut out for arm-to-arm combat and the last time I checked I didn't have an S branded on my shirt to signify I was Superpimp. Right now, more than anything, I wanted my daughter back.

More than I wanted Destiny to be safe and sound.

Even more than *I* wanted to be able to walk out of here alive.

She's fifteen, dammit.

The same age my brother was when he was killed.

With one swift kick, the door explodes open and I race into the darkness with my heart in my throat and the scent of gasoline filling my nostrils.

"Corrine!"

A small beam of light swings toward me and I swear to God that I hear my brother's voice, telling me to duck and shoot in its direction. I do so without hesitation. I hear an *"Aaagh"* a second before something hot blazes into my arm and rockets me back into the wall.

"Shit," I gasp. The motherfucker shot me.

I hear a heavy thud and then a beam of light spins on the floor.

Shit.

I grunt and groan as I roll forward and then struggle to my feet, my grip still tight on my 9. "Corrine!" Weak, I nearly fall back onto the floor. "Corrine!"

I walk deeper into the living room and closer to the spinning flashlight. I hear a strange wheezing and know that it's Demarcus struggling for his last few seconds of life.

Still coughing my damn self, I lean down and stop the spinning flashlight. Because of the growing fire, I'm able to meet Demarcus Jones's stare.

He's looking at me as if confused or rather like he's staring at a ghost. The smallest of smiles curls his lips as his gun tumbles out of his hand and he tries to speak.

"I—I'm. Glad. It. Was. You."

I frown. What the fuck is this mutherfucker talkin' about? Though my shoulder feels like it's on fire, I lift the gun in my hand. "Where's my daughter, mother-fucker?"

He doesn't answer but his eyes shift to the left.

I follow his gaze, swinging the flashlight's beam toward two bodies sprawled across the floor, lifeless.

At that moment, it feels like someone opened my chest and ripped out my heart.

"K-Kadrian," Demarcus choked.

My attention jerks back toward him. "What the fuck did you just say?"

"He. Was. Walking. Alone." He licked his lips. "I. Had. To. Shoot . . ."

This nigga killed my brother, too?!

I don't know what kind of warped *Twilight Zone* shit this is, but I lift my 9 and aim to permanently put him to sleep.

"D-do it," he whispers. "P-please."

"Ain't no need to beg, punk motherfucker!" I squeeze the trigger and watch my bullet slam into his forehead.

"Burn in hell."

Ignoring the pain in my arm, somehow I manage to get over toward the bodies and scoop my daughter into my arms. I stumble more than I walk back out to the car where a panicked Anderson is screaming into his cell phone for help. When Renee sees me, she launches out of the back of the Bentley with her eyes wide.

She races toward me in her red gown and falls to her knees next to me and Corrine. "Oh my God. Oh my God," she cries. Her hands shake as she reaches out to touch Corrine's still figure, but there's a river flowing from her eyes when she looks up at me.

"Oh baby, I'm so sorry."

I completely break down. Corrine's death has destroyed me to my core. She just wanted to be wanted . . . to be loved. And I'd failed to let her know how much I wanted her. Tears pour down my face as I allow my wife to pull me into her embrace. I clutch her tight, stealing her warmth until I can feel a calm settle over me.

"Baby, we're going to get through this," she promises.

I close my eyes. I'll never recover from this.

"You'll see," she tells me.

I nod as I lean forward and press my lips against hers. She tastes so sweet and feels so good.

I'm gonna miss her.

"I love you," I whisper and then press my 9 against her stomach and quickly pull the trigger. She jerks in my arms and I pull back to break our kiss. She blinks up at me with her tears still sliding down her face. I move in close to her ear and whisper, "You were always gonna be my number one girl."

30

The Dealer

I open my eyes and everything around me is dark. Almost like I am blind.

I see visions of my son laughing up at me.

Visions of my mother touching the back of my head in the mornings before she walked me out the door to school.

Visions of Dad taking me fishing on Saturday mornings.

Visions of Quilla smiling up at me just before she tells me she loves me.

People who will truly miss me when I'm gone.

After a few seconds of adjustment I can make out that I'm still sitting in the same spot in the living room. My body aches all over and I wish like hell having my arms tied behind my back didn't pull on my gunshot wound. I can smell my own blood and I know it reopened.

"Fuck that, Spyce, its time we kill that mark-ass nigga just like we planned from the jump."

I frown at the sound of voices coming down the short hall from the bedroom.

"You finished countin' and baggin' up our shit?"

"There's fifty grand in money and a hundred grand in weight just like Usher said."

I wince as the twins laugh like two cackling hens.

"We 'bout to run this shit for real."

"Hol-la!"

The twins are behind everything? Did they have this shit in the works when they caught my eye in the club? Did Usher recruit them or they did recruit him?

I lift my head to look over at his dead body. My friend is dead but it doesn't matter because the moment he pointed a gun at me he was dead to me anyway. He created this bullshit and got himself killed. He dug a hole for me and fell into a six-foot-deep one himself. Karma is and always will be a bitch.

"I am gonna miss the way that nigga eat pussy."

"Which one?"

"Fuck it . . . both!"

They laugh again and my fists clench because I can just imagine how they would feel with my hands around their neck. Pussy was my downfall. I don't have time to marinate on how pussy got me in the game. I got to think and free myself from this motherfucker. I'm not dyin' in no shitty-ass Bentley Manor. My life ain't start that way and it damn sure ain't gone end that way. I fight the pain and try to free my hands of the ties.

"What we gone do with these bodies?" one twin asks.

"Fuck it, we'll leave 'em here. Word already hot on the street that somebody tried to kill him at that bitch's funeral. They ain't even tryna check for two bitches doing it."

"Damn straight."

I feel anxious. I don't want to die.

I feel frustrated. I want to kill.

I knuckle up and work that scarf down my wrists. It feels like I'm going to snap my wrist. I bite my lip. Pain shoots through my ribs, my back, my shoulder. I close my eyes as I concentrate.

CLICK.

Next I feel the cold metal of the gun pressed to my forehead as my hands are untied.

"Get the fuck up," one of the twins orders me in a hard voice.

When I don't move fast enough for these bitches the gun presses deeper into my flesh. At least with my hands free again and Usher dead I can try to make a power move of my own against these psycho bitches. For whatever reason they hadn't smoked me like they did Usher. I have to take that to my advantage.

I'm not dying tonight.

In the bathroom, I carefully hid a piece inside the toilet's tank. Nice and dry inside a Ziploc bag is a 9mm and a silencer. Maleek believed when you look for a hiding spot to not overlook the obvious. When he first gave me that gun I laughed it off and it's been floating in the tank ever since. I have to get to it.

It's just waitin' on me. Waitin' for the right time.

It's a dog-eat-dog world and Usher always tried to teach me to kill or be killed.

Humph. Who knew that ugly motherfucker was so right?

They shove me down the hall to the bedroom. The gun is now pressed to the back of my head.

I pause when we near the bathroom door. I tense up to duck from the gun and elbow one of these bitches. Just long enough to get inside the bathroom to get at that gun.

"Don't try nothin'," is whispered into my ear in a hard voice.

As we near it I hear moaning. I frown.

What are these bitches up to now?

"Kas . . . Kas . . . help me. Help me, Kas."

Quilla?

I step into the bedroom and the sight of Quilla naked, beaten, and bruised almost beyond recognition, makes my hands literally itch to choke these bitches. She is tied to the bed, blood staining the sheets from her wounds.

One of the twins pushes past me to walk into the room. "We all had a good time, but not a good as your *queen,*"

Suga says sarcastically as she waves her hand at Quilla's body. "The pussy taste real good."

Spyce laughs as Suga bends down to swipe her tongue across Quilla's clit. I ain't no killa but don't try me.

Enough is enough.

I duck my head, turn, and grab Spyce's hand while I drag that no good bitch into the hall with me. She tries to struggle against me but I punch her dead in the face and snatch the gun from her grasp. She falls to the floor like there isn't a bone in her body.

No-good bitch.

"I'll kill your bitch if your hurt my sister," Suga yells out from inside the bedroom.

I look down at the gun. Feel the weight of it in my hand. Tried to imagine myself using it. Can I take a life— two lives—in cold blood? I never been about this type of gangsta shit. Never.

With the gun raised I step back inside the room. She has a gun pointed at Quilla's head.

It's a crazy time for it to hit home that I love Quilla. I mean really love her. I'd rather die trying to save her than leave her behind. She is my woman and tonight I will be her savior.

"Y'all put me in this spot, Suga," I tell her as I step closer to the bed.

"What spot?" she asks.

"Kill or be killed."

I fire and my hand jolts. The silencer works and there

is only a low and brief sound of the bullet leaving the gun and whizzing across the room to enter Suga's heart. She gasps sharply as the impact sends her flying backward. A red strain is spreading fast as hell from her chest as she hits the wall.

"NO!"

I whirl around just as Spyce fires a shot. The bullet flies past my shoulder and Quilla cries out sharply behind me. In an automatic reaction I fire off two bullets at Spyce. One hits her shoulder and the other pierces her head between her eyes.

I'm not no killa but don't try me.

Life goes on.

These motherfuckers asked for this and now I gotta to do what I gotta do. With one last look at their dead bodies piled on the bed, I cover them with my one-thousand-count sheet and then toss a book of lit matches on top of their corpses. I stand there with my bag of money at my feet and watch the fire engulf their bodies in the abandoned apartment at the rear of the building.

I dragged them motherfuckers right on down there and took my time cleaning up Olive's apartment because I didn't want the murders traced back to her . . . or to me. With no furniture or curtains to catch fire it would be a minute before it spread, and that should crisp them murderous assholes right on up.

For good measure, I broke the sprinklers throughout the apartment.

Once I smell burning flesh I know I have to bounce. I toss the last of the crack cocaine into the fire. Let them burn with what they treasured. With one last look, I turn and limp my ass out the apartment. I walk back into Olive's apartment and scoop up Quilla's blanket-covered body into my arms. I give myself a moment to press my face into her neck as she fights through the pain haze to wrap her arms around my neck.

"I love you, Kas," she whispers near my chin.

My heart feels like someone is squeezing it inside their fist. "I love you too, Quilla. I love the hell out of you."

Thank God the bullet went into her thigh. I had it wrapped tight to stop the bleeding. My moms would be able to take out the bullet and stitch her up. I still had to come up with a lie for why my girl got shot.

With one last look around the apartment I leave it for the last time. Fuck Bentley Manor and the dope game. I'm out.

Lola and her kids aren't home but for good measure, on my way out the door, I grab the fire alarm and pull it.

That will alert people that they need to haul ass with a quickness.

All is clear when I walk out the building and put Quilla in the passenger seat before I hop into the little bullshit car that had paper tags. I pull out of Bentley Manor. As I turn the corner, I look in my rearview mirror and can see the flames engulfing the rear apartment on the second floor.

I ain't no killa but don't try me.

Epilogue

Miz Osceola

Atlanta burns again.

I reach over and grab Cleo's hand as we stand among the rest of the crowd outside the gates of Bentley Manor. Gone are the images of brick to be replaced by walls of flame. Right now, it's just one building burning and the firefighters are struggling to keep it that way.

I can't help but shift my eyes from that building on fire to my own building just a hundred feet away. "Lord, please," I pray in a little whisper.

Cleo clutches my hand a little tighter. I look over at her and it hurt to see the same sadness and fear I feel. It pains me to see the reflection of the fire in her eyes.

Bentley Manor has many faults: drugs, murder, and crime, but it's also a family and like any family you take the good with the bad. And there is good here. Families have been raised here. Lives have begun here. People have started a life here and then moved on to bigger and better things, but the first step right here in the projects was the most important part of folks getting they act together. We look out for each other here and do for each other here.

And me and Cleo feel a little less lonely here.

This is all we know. This is all some people got.

"This is Heather Oakley reporting from the scene of a horrible fire at the Bentley Manor projects . . ."

I look over at a newswoman from my favorite news program talking into a camera. I can't get excited though, because she here—they all here—because our home is burning down before our eyes.

I tune her out. I ain't got time to think 'bout no other fire. I'm worried like the dickens about my home. My friends. My precious items that can't be replaced. Cleo and I grabbed as much as we could before the buildings were evacuated but we left so much behind.

And what will become of Bentley Manor?

If the fire spreads, will it be rebuilt? Will we all have to find new holes to get in?

I can't stop the tears that fill my eyes. Cleo wraps her arms around mine tight. "We gone be all right, friend," she tells me.

"Yes, 'cause God is good."

"All the time," she answers softly just as the fire seems to get bigger and brighter.

"All the time," I respond.

"God is good."

Still, I'm afraid. I'm very afraid. I can't explain why this feels like the end of Bentley Manor to me.

God help us all.

Acknowledgments

During life, God puts special people in your path to help guide you toward your destiny. I have truly been blessed and I thank them all:

Mama: my angel (while you were here on earth and now while you're in heaven)

Tony: my backbone.

Caleb: my protector.

Kal-El and Hajah: my inner joy.

The Johnson and Bryant family: my reality check.

Claudia: my advisor.

Meghan, Sulay, Jamie, Shida, Shawna, and the entire Touchstone team: my own entourage—kinda sorta (smile).

All of the readers: my will 2 keep writing.

The bookstores, book clubs, and reviewers: my support.

Those who will continue to step into my path and help me get where I am destined to be: my future.

Blessings,

Meesha

Dear God, there are no words to express my love and appreciation for all that you have given me. Your unconditional and everlasting love endures and strengthens me. To every angel I've lost here on earth (with two legs and with four), it makes me smile to know that you're now watching me from above. To my sisters, Channon and Charla, I'm proud of the women you two have become. To my three-year-old niece Courtney—you're my best friend too. To my mom, despite our difference, I'll always love you.

My best friend, Kathy, I love you despite your being a Republican. To Charles—there's no better man to take care of my best friend. To my second family, the Barretts—you've meant so much to me over the years.

To the Byrdwatchers fan club: What a great group of women you are. Thanks for your encouragement, your exuberant support, and love.

To my favorite cousin, Josephine Johnson. I don't know what I'd do without our nightly chats. To the men and women I've met working on the Barack Obama campaign—YES WE CAN!

To my sisters of the written word, Tu-shonda Whitaker and Melanie Schuster, ladies, you kept me sane during this process. I thank you so much for that. To Meghan Stevenson, I had a wonderful time working with you. And most of all, to all the readers of the *Hoodwives* series: thanks so much for the thousands of letters and e-mails. I'm so pleased to be a part of something that was both entertaining and educational. As women, always remember to love and respect yourself first—and always WRAP IT UP.

—De'nesha

About the Authors

Meesha Mink is the pseudonym for Niobia Bryant, a national bestselling and award-winning author with over ten works in print in multiple genres for multiple publishing houses (Kensington/Dafina, Harlequin, and Simon & Schuster/Touchstone). The HOODWIVES series is her first collection of sexy urban fiction but definitely not her last. Currently the author splits her time between her hometown of Newark, New Jersey, and her second home in South Carolina. For more on Meesha visit www. myspace.com/meeshamink and for more on the author's works under her real name visit www.niobiabryant.com. E-mail her directly at meesha.mink@yahoo.com.

De'nesha Diamond is the pseudonym for Adrianne Byrd, a national bestselling author of thirty novels. Adrianne Byrd has always preferred to live within the realms of her imagination where all the men are gorgeous and the women are worth whatever trouble they manage to get into. As an army brat, she traveled throughout Europe and learned to appreciate and value different cultures. Now she calls Georgia home. For more information on De'nesha Diamond and Adrianne Byrd's work visit www.adriannebyrd.com or www.deneshadiamond.com

For more on the explosive HOODWIVES series
visit the official Web site:
www.HOODWIVES.com
or the HOODWIVES MySpace page:
www.myspace.com/minkanddiamond